EVOLUTION

HOW LIFE ADAPTS TO A CHANGING ENVIRONMENT

WITH **25 PROJECTS**

CARLA MOONEY
ILLUSTRATED BY ALEXIS CORNELL

~ More science titles in the *Build It Yourself* series ~

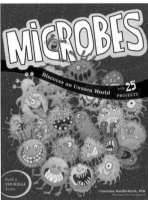
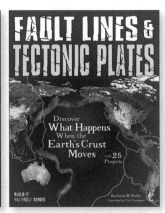

Check out more titles at www.nomadpress.net

Nomad Press
A division of Nomad Communications
10 9 8 7 6 5 4 3 2 1

This book was manufactured by Versa Press
East Peoria, Illinois
November 2017, Job # J17-08780

ISBN Softcover: 978-1-61930-601-1
ISBN Hardcover: 978-1-61930-597-7

Educational Consultant, Marla Conn

Questions regarding the ordering of this book should be addressed to
Nomad Press
2456 Christian St.
White River Junction, VT 05001
www.nomadpress.net

Printed in the United States.

CONTENTS

Interested in Primary Sources?

Look for this icon. Use a smartphone or tablet app to scan the QR code and explore more! You can find a list of URLs on the Resources page. If the QR code doesn't work, try searching the Internet with the Keyword Prompts to find other helpful sources.

evolution 🔍

TIMELINE

1735: Carolus Linnaeus publishes *Systema Naturae*, which includes the common system of naming species with two names.

1764: The fossilized bones of a large animal later named "Mosasaur" are found in a quarry in the Netherlands.

1809: Jean-Baptiste Lamarck, a French naturalist, publishes his theory of evolution.

1811: Mary Anning discovers the fossilized remains of an ichthyosaur in England. Ichthyosaurs are giant marine reptiles that look like fish and dolphins.

1812: Paleontologist Georges Cuvier argues the distribution of fossils in the rock record proves fossils occur in the order of creation: fish, amphibians, reptiles, and mammals.

1818: William Charles Wells conveys his principle of natural selection among human populations and suggests that African populations are selected for their resistance to local diseases.

1818: Étienne Geoffroy Saint-Hilaire develops the idea of homologous parts and argues that parts such as a bat's wing and a man's arm have the same evolutionary origin, but serve different functions.

1831: Darwin begins a five-year voyage on the *HMS Beagle*. He studies differences among mockingbirds in the Galapagos Islands, his first examination of the evolution of species.

1838–1839: Darwin develops his theory of natural selection. He argues that favorable traits become more common in successive generations.

1848: A skull that would come to be known as Neanderthal Man is discovered in Gibraltar, England.

1856: Fossils found at Neanderthal in the Neander Valley near Dusseldorf, Germany, are identified as an early variant of *Homo sapiens*.

1859: Darwin publishes *On the Origin of Species*.

1866: Gregor Mendel publishes *Experiments in Plant Hybridization*, which becomes a foundational work for the study of biology.

1871: Darwin publishes *The Descent of Man* and applies evolution to humans.

TIMELINE

1886: Two complete Neanderthal skeletons are found in a cave near Spy, Belgium. The skeletons challenge the idea that Neanderthals are modern humans.

1891: Scientists discover remains on the island of Java that would be later classified as *Homo erectus*.

1907: Chemist Bertram Boltwood measures the ratio of isotopes of uranium and lead in a mineral and lays the groundwork for radiometric dating techniques.

1931: Scientist Sewall Wright concludes that random drift, or chance fluctuation of gene populations, is a significant factor in evolution.

1936: Robert Broom discovers the first adult *Australopithecus* at Sterkfontein, South Africa, and establishes it as an early hominin.

1953: James Watson, Francis Crick, and Maurice Wilkins publish the first accurate model of DNA structure, based on Rosalina Franklin's pioneering image of DNA taken in 1952.

1960: Louis and Mary Leakey discover *Homo habilis* at Olduvai Gorge in Tanzania. *Homo habilis* is believed to be the first species of the genus *Homo*.

1967: Scientists publish a time scale for human evolution, placing the split between chimpanzees and humans at about 5 million years ago.

1974: Donald Johanson recovers the skeletal remains of a female hominin dated to 2.8 million years ago. His team describes her as a new species, *Australopithecus afarensis*, and nicknames the female hominid "Lucy."

1984: The study of evolution at the DNA level begins.

1987: Scientists develop a genealogical tree that suggests all human DNA can be traced back to a common African ancestor.

1994: In Ethiopia, American paleoanthropologist Tim D. White and colleagues discover a human ancestor, *Ardipithecus ramidus*, dating to 4.4 million years ago.

2004: *Homo floresiensis*, a type of dwarf human, is discovered on the Indonesian island of Flores and is announced as a new species.

2015: Scientists discover the fossils of a new species of early human, which they name *Homo naledi*.

WHAT IS
EVOLUTION?

Millions of years ago, life on Earth was nothing like it is today. Dinosaurs roamed the earth and pterosaurs flew through the skies. Even trees and plants were larger or smaller or had different shapes than they do now—some of the varieties that flourished back then no longer exist. Millions of years before the dinosaurs, life was even more different. Strange ocean creatures lived in the seas, while the land had no life at all.

Throughout its history, Earth has been home to an incredible **diversity** of living things. As the world has changed, living things have **adapted** and changed dramatically during hundreds of millions of years. How have these living creatures changed? And how did that change happen? **Evolution**!

1

WORDS TO KNOW

diversity: a range of different things.

adapt: to change in order to survive.

evolution: the process of living things gradually changing to adapt to the world around them.

biology: the study of life and living things.

organism: any living thing, such as a plant or animal.

environment: a natural area with animals, plants, rocks, soil, and water.

mutation: a permanent change in an organism's DNA.

genetic: traits that are passed from parent to child in the DNA.

DNA: deoxyribonucleic nucleic acid. Genetic material that contains instructions that make us who we are.

cell: the most basic part of a living thing. Billions of cells make up a plant or animal.

gene: a section of DNA that codes for a particular trait.

protein: a group of large molecules. Proteins are an essential part of all living things.

characteristic: a feature or trait.

reproduce: to make more of something.

generation: a group born and living at about the same time.

offspring: a plant's or animal's young.

chromosome: the part of a cell that contains genes.

WORDS TO KNOW

One of the most important ideas in **biology**, evolution explains why there are so many different living **organisms** on Earth. It also explains why you are the way you are.

Evolution is the process by which populations of living things change throughout time.

Because of evolution, you walk on two legs and communicate with language. And although evolution is the story of our past, it also helps us understand our future and how we continue to evolve.

A POWERFUL PROCESS

Evolution is an important and powerful process. During the course of billions of years, evolution favors the organisms that are best adapted to their changing **environments**.

The process relies on changes, called **mutations**, in an organism's **genetic** material. Every living thing on Earth, from the smallest insect to the largest elephant, has a chemical molecule called **DNA** in its **cells**. DNA stores genetic information. It is like an instruction manual that holds the information an organism needs to grow and function.

The shape of DNA is called a double helix. Segments of DNA called **genes** code the instructions for making a cell's **proteins**. These proteins determine an organism's **characteristics** and enable it to live and grow.

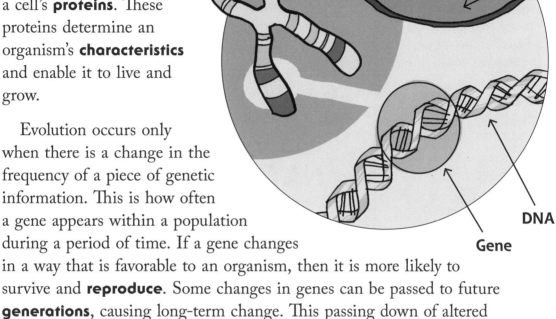

Chromosome

Cell

DNA

Gene

Evolution occurs only when there is a change in the frequency of a piece of genetic information. This is how often a gene appears within a population during a period of time. If a gene changes in a way that is favorable to an organism, then it is more likely to survive and **reproduce**. Some changes in genes can be passed to future **generations**, causing long-term change. This passing down of altered genes from parent to **offspring** is an important part of evolution.

DNA and Chromosomes

An organism's DNA is located in a structure within a cell called a **chromosome**. Some organisms have only one chromosome. Others have many. Plants and animals have pairs of chromosomes. Each parent contributes one set of chromosomes to their offspring. Humans have 23 pairs of chromosomes. One set came from your mom, while the other set came from your dad. This means that half your genes came from your mom, and half from your dad.

While evolution happens gradually through time, it does not always occur at a steady rate. Sometimes, genes and gene frequencies stay the same for many, many years. Other times, the environment changes and organisms are forced to adapt. The genetic information within genes that give organisms an **advantage** in the changed environment are more likely to be passed to offspring. The genes will increase in the population, while genes that are unfavorable might decrease.

NATURAL SELECTION

In the 1800s, a British scientist named Charles Darwin (1809-1882) came up with an idea about evolution. When studying different plant and animal **species**, Darwin noticed that the offspring were different from the parents in various ways. They were **variable**. Some characteristics from the parents were passed from one generation to the next, while other characteristics were not. He wanted to understand how this happened. What decided which characteristics would be passed from parent to offspring?

Based on his observations, Darwin believed that some offspring would have an advantage over others at surviving and reproducing. He concluded that the characteristics that improved survival and reproduction could be passed from parent to offspring. As time passed, the favorable characteristics would be passed in increasing numbers to offspring. Eventually, it would lead to changes in the population.

Darwin called his idea **natural selection**. Darwin explained that natural selection is the way changes in an organism are passed to later generations. Not every organism in a generation has the same chance of passing genes to the next generation. Some are favored, while others are not.

Darwin suspected that natural selection works the same way as **artificial selection**. This is a process used by farmers in **breeding**. By choosing chickens that lay more eggs or flowers that are brighter and last longer to reproduce, we can produce superior products. Darwin realized that if humans could affect a species by artificial selection, the natural world could also make changes to a species during a longer period of time. This is what he called natural selection.

Micro vs. Macro Evolution

Scientists think about evolution on two time scales—microevolution and macroevolution. Microevolution is evolution of one population during a short time period, which results in small changes. An example of microevolution is a mutation in a **bacterium** gene that allows it to grow and divide faster than other, similar bacteria. Because of its short timeframe, scientists can observe microevolution.

Macroevolution is evolution across many species during a long period of time. It's the same process as microevolution, but takes longer to occur. Macroevolution consists of the larger changes that scientists study, such as **extinction** or **speciation**.

predator: an animal that hunts another animal for food.

theory: an idea that tries to explain why something is the way it is.

ancestor: someone from your family who lived before you.

WORDS TO KNOW

In natural selection, some favorable characteristics make it more likely that an organism will reproduce and pass its genes on to the next generation. These organisms tend to reproduce more than organisms with negative characteristics.

In several generations, the process of natural selection increases the favorable characteristics in a population, while reducing negative ones. That's evolution at work!

You might see an example of natural selection in a population of gazelles. Some can run very fast, while others are slower. On the African savannahs, gazelles have many **predators**. The gazelles that can run the fastest and escape predators are more likely to survive. These survivors are then more likely to reproduce and pass their speedy genetic information along to their offspring.

Gazelles that run more slowly are more likely to be caught and killed by predators. Their genes are less likely to be passed on to offspring. After a few generations, you'll find fewer slow gazelles.

STILL CHANGING

Think evolution is over? Think again! Evolution is happening all around you. In *Evolution: How Life Adapts to a Changing Environment*, you'll learn about evolution and how every living species evolves to adapt to the changing environment. You'll also explore the **theory** of evolution, its history, how we think it works, examples of creatures that have evolved in response to specific circumstances, and what this might mean for the future of our planet.

The activities in *Evolution* will help you understand the science of evolution. As evolutionary biologists, you will apply these concepts to solve problems and explain the incredibly diverse world around you. Are you ready to take a journey to explore our common **ancestors** and look toward our shared future?

Good Science Practices

Every good scientist keeps a science journal! Scientists use the scientific method to keep their experiments organized. Choose a notebook to use as your science journal. As you read through this book and do the activities, keep track of your observations and record each step in a scientific method worksheet, like the one shown here.

Each chapter of this book begins with an essential question to help guide your exploration of evolution. Keep the question in your mind as you read the chapter. At the end of each chapter, use your science journal to record your thoughts and answers.

Question: What are we trying to find out? What problem are we trying to solve?
Research: What is already known about the problem?
Hypothesis/Prediction: What do we think the answer will be?
Equipment: What supplies are we using?
Method: What procedure are we following?
Results: What happened? Why?

ESSENTIAL QUESTION

What would the world be like if evolution never happened?

Darwin's Finches

In 1835, Charles Darwin visited the Galapagos Islands in the Pacific Ocean. While there, he noticed several different types of finches. These birds were very different from the finches Darwin had seen in England. The finches on the different islands had beaks of various sizes and shapes. A finch's beak structure determines what it can eat most efficiently. A finch with a tiny beak cannot easily crack large seeds. Finches with large beaks have trouble picking up tiny seeds. Darwin suspected the different beaks he observed were related to the finches' feeding. He hypothesized that the different environmental conditions on each island had caused the finch populations to evolve by natural selection.

Today, there are 13 species of finches on the Galapagos Islands. As Darwin hypothesized more than a century ago, many modern scientists believe that one species of finch arrived on the islands and evolved by natural selection to adapt different **traits** to different food sources. In this activity, you are going to demonstrate how different **adaptations** can help different birds collect food.

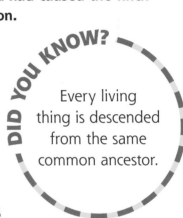

DID YOU KNOW?

Every living thing is descended from the same common ancestor.

❯ **Gather several objects** that represent different types of seeds a bird might encounter, including large seeds, small seeds, dried beans, rice, candies, etc.

❯ **Find or design several "tools"** that you can use to pick up the seeds. You can use traditional tools, such as forks, spoons, knives, chopsticks, tweezers, and straws. You can also build your own tool.

❯ **Using each tool, attempt to pick up each type of seed.** Which tool works the best? What type of seed is the easiest to collect? Which tool is the least effective? Which seed is the hardest to collect? Do some tools work better with certain seeds and not others?

WORDS TO KNOW

trait: a specific characteristic of an organism determined by genes or the environment.

adaptation: a trait that has evolved through natural selection.

❯ **Now consider how changes** in the environment might affect the different beak adaptations.

✱ What would happen if one seed type became more common than the others? How would this affect the population of birds?

✱ What would happen if the plant that was the source of one type of seed died out? How would this affect the population of birds?

✱ Does having a different beak shape increase or decrease competition among the birds for food? Explain.

TRY THIS: Demonstrate the process of evolution by natural selection using the seeds and your tools. Using only one type of food, assign each of the tools to a friend or classmate. Set a time limit and see how many seeds they can collect with their assigned tool. After the time has expired, see which tools have collected the most food. Those that did not collect enough food will die out and be replaced by the top-performing tools. Repeat this process several times. What happens to the tools in the populations? What was the role of natural selection in the outcome?

Chapter 1

HOW DOES EVOLUTION WORK?

If you step outside and take a look at all the different forms of life, what do you see? Birds, ants, humans, grass, trees, and more! How are all of these similar? How are they different? What would the world be like if all life were the same?

Evolution is responsible for both the remarkable **similarities** we see across all life and the amazing diversity of that life. How is this possible? How does evolution happen? Let's take a look.

VARIATION IS THE KEY

Variation is a crucial part of evolution. Without variation, evolution would come to a grinding halt. And we're not talking about any type of variation. The variation necessary for evolution must be able to be passed from parent to offspring.

Every organism in a species is not the same. Think about your classmates. You are all part of the human species. But everyone looks different. Some people are tall, while others are short. Some people have blond hair, while others have brown or red hair. Everyone has different features, skin tones, and eye colors. That's variation.

While some variations, such as height or skin color, are easy to see, other variations are not as noticeable. A person's blood type or whether they have certain diseases, such as diabetes, are also variations. If these differences can be passed from parent to offspring through genes, then they are **heritable** variations.

If everyone had the exact same genetic information in their genes, there would be no change from generation to generation. Imagine every single person on the planet carried the gene for blond hair. They would pass that gene down to their children and grandchildren, resulting in generation after generation of blond-haired people.

Luckily, a lot of variation exists in living things. But where does variation come from?

ESSENTIAL QUESTION

Why is mutation important for evolution?

MUTATIONS

DNA is an incredibly tough molecule. That's a good thing, since it has the important job of holding and protecting the instructions for life! If those instructions were lost, an organism would not be able to function and survive.

However, DNA is not foolproof. Sometimes, mistakes occur in DNA. These mistakes are mutations. Mutations can cause an organism's DNA sequence to be different from that of its parents, making, in effect, a new gene. Because DNA affects how an organism looks, behaves, and works, a change in DNA can cause changes in all parts of life.

Most mutations have no effect on an organism. Some mutations can have a small effect on an organism, such as the mutation that changed eye color from brown to blue. Sometimes mutations can have a significant effect, such as the mutation of a fruit fly that causes a leg to grow on its head instead of an antenna.

Mutations happen all the time. Sometimes, mistakes happen during the process of **DNA replication**. Replication occurs during cell division. During replication, the cell makes a copy of its DNA instructions for a new cell. Sometimes, there are mistakes in the copying that cause a mutation.

Other times, an outside agent damages DNA. This type of damaging agent is called a **mutagen**. Many chemicals are mutagens.

When an organism comes in contact with a mutagen, its DNA can be damaged by that substance.

Although the cell tries to repair the damaged DNA, sometimes, errors remain and become mutations. This can happen to skin cells when they get too much sun.

Not every mutation is important for evolution. Mutations that occur in non-reproductive cells might affect an individual organism, but they will not be passed on to future generations. Only mutations that are heritable matter for evolution. In humans, only mutations that occur in the DNA carried by the female's eggs and the male's sperm can be passed to offspring.

DID YOU KNOW?

Natural selection and adaptations have some limits. Some things will never be possible. For example, no matter how many speedy genes you have, you'll never be able to run 100 miles per hour!

Mutation Effects on Phenotype

A single gene mutation can have several effects. Some changes do not have any noticeable change in an organism's outward appearance and behavior, or its **phenotype**. Some might cause a small change in phenotype, such as creating curly hair. Other mutations can cause a big change in an organism's phenotype. Sometimes, the change can be so big it causes the organism to die. This type of mutation is called a **lethal** mutation.

GENE FLOW

Gene flow, or gene migration, is another factor that can affect the frequency of genes in a population and, therefore, affect evolution. Gene flow, also called **allele** flow, is the movement of individuals and the genetic material they carry from one population to another. Do you have grandparents or great-grandparents who came from a different country? When they moved, they introduced their genes into a new-to-them population. This is an example of gene flow.

Gene flow occurs when people move from one country to another county. It also occurs when pollen from plants blows to a new area. Gene flow occurs when any organism moves to a new population.

Gene flow is the movement of alleles between populations.

Gene flow can be an important part of creating genetic variation. For example, imagine that an insect carrying a gene for brown coloring is introduced to a population of insects that are all green. By adding the brown insect's genes to the population, there is more genetic variation. Genes for brown and green are now in the population.

Have you ever seen plant pollen blowing in the wind? This causes gene flow for these plants.

Sexual reproduction is another way to introduce new gene combinations to a population. During sexual reproduction, the genes from the mother and father are shuffled, creating new combinations of genes. For example, a puppy might have big paws and a long nose because his mother had the genes for big paws and his father had genes for a long nose. Their offspring, the puppy, has a new combination of genes that he can pass on to the next generation.

NATURAL SELECTION

Now that you know what causes variation in a species, let's look at what causes traits to change.

Natural selection is one way that evolution occurs. Natural selection is the process by which some organisms with specific desirable traits, such as keen hearing, reproduce more than organisms without those traits. During the passage of time, if certain traits are favored over others and those traits are heritable, evolution occurs. Across many generations, the frequency of the favorable traits will increase in the population or species. For example, hearing gets sharper because individuals with less-sensitive hearing are not passing along the genes for weaker hearing to their offspring and future generations.

DID YOU KNOW? Natural selection affects more than just appearance. It can also affect behaviors that are genetic, such as bird-mating rituals and the ability to learn language.

What Is Natural Selection?

In natural selection, nature is the selective agent. In artificial selection, humans are the selective agent. Watch this quick video to better understand natural selection.

what is natural selection 🔍

anatomy: the structure of animals, plants, and other living organisms.

echolocation: the ability to find an object by sending out sound waves and listening for them to bounce back.

antibiotic: a type of drug used in the treatment and prevention of bacterial infections.

genetic drift: a change in the gene frequency in a population due to random chance.

WORDS TO KNOW

For natural selection to work, you must have variation in traits.

Consider a population of brown and green insects. Not every insect will be able to reproduce to its full ability. Some will be eaten by birds. In this example, assume that the green insects show up better to the birds than the brown insects. That means the birds are more likely to eat the green ones. The brown insects have offspring that are also brown—it is a genetic trait. Because there are more brown insects, they will have more offspring than the green insects. Over time, the favorable trait of brown color will become more common in the insect population. Eventually, most of the insects will be brown.

ADAPTATIONS

The results of natural selection are called adaptations. An adaptation is a trait that results from evolution by natural selection. It can take many forms. An adaptation can be a behavior that allows an organism to better avoid predators. Remember the speedy gazelles from the introduction of this book? The ability of gazelles to run fast is an example of this type of adaptation.

Other adaptations might help an organism better regulate its body temperature. A change in an organism's **anatomy** might allow it to better reach food. For example, **echolocation** in bats is an adaptation that helps them catch insects.

Antibiotic Resistance

The discovery of **antibiotics** in 1928 to treat bacterial infections was a breakthrough in medicine. Since then, some bacteria have developed antibiotic resistance. They are able to survive and reproduce even in the presence of antibiotics. This antibiotic resistance is an adaptation. It appeared in bacteria as the result of a random mutation. The bacteria with this mutation were better able to survive and pass this genetic mutation on to the next generation. Through time, the trait has increased in bacteria population. More bacteria have become antibiotic resistant.

CHANGE BY CHANCE: GENETIC DRIFT

The main idea of natural selection is that the environment favors traits that make an individual organism better able to survive and pass its genes on to the next generation. Parents who are more fit pass their genes to their offspring, who are then also more fit. The cycle continues and the fit genes are passed along so that these traits increase in frequency in future generations.

Natural selection is not the only force that determines what genes make it to the next generation. Sometimes, a random event can come along and change everything! This idea is called **genetic drift**.

DID YOU KNOW?

While mutations that create genetic variation are random, natural selection is not random. Genetic information that helps organisms survive and reproduce are more likely to be passed to offspring and become more common in a population.

WORDS TO KNOW

prey: an animal hunted by another animal.

fitness: how successful an organism is at passing its genes to its offspring.

genotype: an organism's genes for a trait.

WORDS TO KNOW

Think about what happens if a forest fire wipes out most of the red-blooming flowers in a particular area. In future generations, there will be fewer red-flowering plants. In the same way, a lightning strike could kill the fastest lion before it's able to pass those fast genes along to offspring. In addition, there might be more **prey** for slower lions to eat, enabling them to survive and have more offspring than they might have otherwise.

Even the number of offspring an organism has can be random. If two organisms are equally able to survive in an environment, only chance will determine which one has more offspring and passes on more genes to future generations. In this way, genetic drift can impact evolution.

What is Fitness?

So how does **fitness** affect evolution? When talking about evolution, fitness is not how fast you can run a mile. In evolutionary biology, fitness describes how successful an organism is at passing its genes to its offspring. For example, if black beetles consistently have more offspring than green beetles because of their black color, the black beetles would have a higher fitness. The fittest organisms are not necessarily the strongest, fastest, or largest. Instead, fitness refers to an organism's ability to survive and reproduce, passing its genes to the future generations.

Genotype vs. Phenotype

There are two types of variations in living things. Phenotype variations are differences in outward physical traits. A **genotype** variation is a difference in the underlying genetic code. Sometimes, two individuals that look the same, or have the same phenotype, have different genotypes. And individuals with the same genotype can have different phenotypes. For example, a person's height is affected by both genetic and environmental factors. A person's genes hold instructions for how much they should grow, but if they don't eat well, their body might not be able to support this growth. That's why two identical twins with the exact same genes might be different heights if environmental factors such as diet affected one of them. And, you might be the same height as your friend, but you don't have the same genes. Natural selection uses phenotypes, the outward characteristics that an organism has to help it survive. But if those phenotypes are not matched in the genotype, or genes, then the characteristic will not be passed along to the next generation.

Any environmental factor that affects an individual organism's ability to reproduce can cause genetic drift.

A forest fire or a flood does not affect the genes of individual organisms, but it can affect the frequency of those genes in future generations. Organisms killed by random events won't be reproducing. Their genes will not be passed to future generations. In this way, random events can change the frequency of certain genes in future generations.

In a larger population, the impact of genetic drift is usually not felt very much. If there are a lot of fast lions, the death of one isn't going to make much of a difference in the number of fast genes passed to future generations. But in a small population, genetic drift can have a real impact. As a population gets smaller, it loses diversity. Genetic drift can reduce and even eliminate genetic diversity in a small population, which can put the population at risk. A new disease that attacks one individual can likely attack all if there is little genetic diversity.

WORDS TO KNOW

coevolution: when a change in one species causes a change in another species.

mutualistic coevolution: when two species evolve together, with the changes benefitting both.

parasite: an animal or plant that lives on or in another plant or animal, feeding off of it, without any benefit to the host.

host: an animal or plant from which a parasite or other organism gets nutrition.

EVOLVING TOGETHER: COEVOLUTION

Sometimes, two or more species affect each other's evolution. This process is called **coevolution**. A change in one species causes a change in another species. For example, a change in the form or structure of a plant could affect the animal that eats the plant. The resulting change in the animal might cause another change in the plant, which again affects the animal, and so on.

Coevolution generally happens when two species interact closely. Coevolution between mutually benefitting species is called **mutualistic coevolution**.

Some moths and orchids are an example of mutualistic coevolution. A species of moth called Morgan's sphinx moth has a tongue that is almost 12 inches long. Why does this moth have such a long tongue? Because of the flower it feeds on, Darwin's orchid.

DID YOU KNOW?

Mutations do not occur because of changes in the environment. They already exist in the population. When a new environmental factor occurs that makes the mutation favorable, then organisms with that mutation are more likely to survive and reproduce than organisms that do not have the mutation.

Like other flowers, Darwin's orchid relies on animals to pick up its pollen and deliver it to other flowers. This process, called pollination, allows the orchid to reproduce. However, most animals cannot reach the nectar in Darwin's orchid because it is located 10 inches down inside a long, thin flower. The only animal that can reach this nectar is the Morgan's sphinx moth—because of its long tongue.

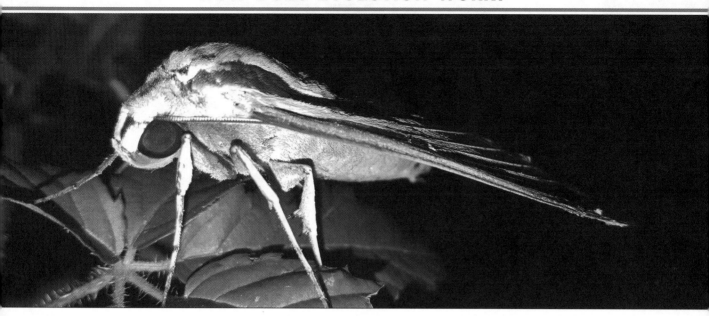

Morgan's sphinx moth

Moths and orchids coevolved to benefit each other. The orchids with shorter nectar tubes were not able to reproduce as much, because the moths coming to drink the nectar were too far away from the flower to pollinate it. So the orchids with longer tubes were more likely to reproduce. At the same time, the sphinx moths with the longest tongues were best able to feed, survive, and reproduce. The long-tongue genes got passed to future generations. As time passed, the sphinx moths got longer tongues to better reach the orchid's nectar. At the same time, the orchids evolved with longer tubes so that the moths could come close enough while feeding to touch the flower to pollinate it.

Coevolution can also occur among species that have negative effects on each other, such as predators and prey or **parasites** and **hosts**.

If an organism passes a mutation down to its offspring, what happens to the species as a whole? Do they all change or do just some of the organisms change? Now that we know something about how evolution works, let's take a look at a very important part of evolution—speciation. This is the way some members of a species become an entirely new species.

ESSENTIAL QUESTION

Now it's time to consider and discuss the Essential Question: Why is mutation important for evolution?

21

Useful Adaptations

Living things adapt to their environment to survive. An adaptation is a change in structure or behavior that allows a species to better survive in its environment. For example, giraffes have long necks to reach the leaves of tall trees. Frogs have long, sticky tongues to catch insects. Plants also adapt to their environments. Cacti store water because they live in dry environments, where water is scarce. The flowers on a rose bush attract bees and butterflies, which allow the plant to reproduce.

Different adaptations are helpful in different environments. For example, white fur is beneficial to an animal living in the Arctic, as the white color in the snow helps it avoid being seen by predators. An animal living in the woods, however, might be better off with brown fur to blend into the forest. In this activity, you will create your own animal with useful adaptations.

❭ **To begin, decide what conditions** your animal will live in. Think about the following questions.

* Where does the animal live?

* How much water is in the area?

* What is the **climate** and weather like in this location?

* What does the animal eat?

* What predators threaten the animal?

❭ **Using these details, create your animal.** What does it look like? How does it behave? Write a paragraph describing your animal and its behaviors. Draw a picture of the animal. What adaptations does the animal have to help it better survive in its environment?

TRY THIS: Design another environment. Imagine your animal in the new environment. What features are useful for the animal in the new environment? What features are not helpful? If the animal stays in the new environment, what new adaptations do you predict will arise during many generations? Why?

WORDS TO KNOW

climate: the weather conditions in an area in general or during a long period of time.

Natural Selection

Natural selection is the process by which some organisms with certain traits that help them better adapt to their environment tend to survive and produce more offspring. In this activity, you will demonstrate how natural selection works.

You will need three types of beans. Each should be a different color. You'll need about 50 beans per type. You'll also need two different colored backgrounds, such as colored paper.

❭ **Spread all of the beans** onto one colored background. Close your eyes for about 30 seconds. Open them and pick up the first bean your eye is drawn to. Close your eyes again for 10 seconds and repeat. Repeat 20 times.

❭ **Count the remaining beans** on the background. Count the beans removed.

❭ **Create a chart** like the one below that shows how many of each bean you removed.

	Bean 1	Bean 2	Bean 3
Round 1			
Round 2			

❭ **Repeat all steps** using the second colored background. Create a data chart for your results.

❭ **Based on your results,** think about the following questions.

✱ On background #1, which bean survived the best? Which bean was the worst survivor? Why do you think this happened? Predict what will happen to this population of beans over time. Explain your prediction.

✱ On background #2, which bean survived the best? Which bean survived the worst? Was this a different result than background #1? Why?

✱ Why do different beans survive better on different backgrounds?

✱ How does this activity simulate natural selection?

TRY THIS: Is there a background/environment in which none of the beans would have an advantage? Why? How would this affect natural selection? Explain.

Survival of the Sweetest

Every individual has unique traits. Sometimes, those traits can give an organism an advantage and help them survive. Other times, a trait has no effect on an organism's survival or can even be a disadvantage. Characteristics that are advantageous are passed down through a population by natural selection. In this activity, you will use candy to replicate the process of natural selection.

❯ **Fill a bowl** with several different types of candy, including popular and unpopular kinds. Record what types of candy and how many pieces of each type are in the bowl. Then, pass the bowl around your classroom and have each student select a piece of candy.

Type	Starting Amount	End Amount	Traits
Tootsie Roll	12	2	chocolate, gooey

❯ **Discuss the traits** of the candies that the students selected from the bowl. Why did they choose the ones they did? Did they pick based on flavor, size, favorite brand, or something else? Create a list of traits for each candy.

❯ **Now, discuss the traits** of the candies that the students did not pick from the bowl. Was the candy too small? Did it taste bad? Create a list of these traits.

❯ **How does this activity simulate natural selection?** Which traits were advantageous for the candy's survival in the bowl? Which were not advantageous?

CONSIDER THIS: What will happen to the candies in the bowl over several generations? Explain. Can you create a system where each piece of candy left in the bowl reproduces with each generation?

Chapter 2

SPECIES AND
SPECIATION

Simply put, evolution is the change in gene frequencies in a group of organisms over time. If enough of these changes occur in one population of a certain species, it could evolve into a new species.

Evolutionary biologists study this process, called speciation, to learn more about evolution. Before you study how one species evolves into two, it's helpful to understand exactly what a species is. Scientists like to group things together to study them. These groups usually are made up of organisms that look or act alike. This allows scientists to study animals, plants, and other organisms based on their similarities.

? ESSENTIAL QUESTION

Why are there different paths to speciation? Why is speciation important to continued life on Earth?

WORDS TO KNOW

classify: to put things in groups based on what they have in common.

fertile: able to produce or reproduce.

infertile: not able to produce or reproduce.

asexual reproduction: to reproduce without mating.

WHAT IS A SPECIES?

To put living organisms in different groups, scientists developed a system to **classify** them. This system places all organisms into groups based on their form, genetic similarity, body chemistry, development, and behavior. These groups start out very large, with lots of organisms in them. The groups get smaller and more specific, with the organisms becoming more alike. The smallest group of organisms that are alike is a species.

A species is a group of organisms that can mate and produce offspring that are also able to reproduce.

DID YOU KNOW? Scientists estimate there are 8.7 million species of living organisms on Earth.

For example, imagine you are the proud owner of a purebred Labrador retriever. One day, your dog escapes from the yard and goes to visit the neighbor's beagle dog. A few months later, the neighbor's dog has an adorable litter of Labrador retriever-beagle puppies. After being adopted into good homes, the puppies grow up and have their own litters of puppies. Your dog is now a grandpa!

The dogs are an example of a species. Even though the Labrador retriever and beagle look very different, they are able to mate and produce **fertile** offspring. According to the biological definition, this makes the two dogs part of the same species.

Now, imagine that you live on a farm with a pet donkey. Your dad decides to breed the donkey with his horse so that he can have a hardworking mule for the farm. After the mule is born, you think it would be a great idea to breed it with another mule, so you have can a bunch of mules on the farm.

HORSE (fertile) + DONKEY (fertile) = MULE (infertile)

But this time, nothing happens. What went wrong? There are no baby mules because even though donkeys and horses can mate and produce offspring, their offspring, the mule, is **infertile**. It cannot mate with other mules to produce its own offspring. This shows that donkeys and horses are different species.

DEFINING SPECIES FOR BACTERIA

The basic definition of a species works best for organisms that reproduce through sexual reproduction. This includes most plants and animals. However, there are lots of organisms in nature where it is a little more difficult to apply this definition.

For example, many bacteria reproduce through **asexual reproduction**, or without mating. Each bacterium divides itself into two daughter bacteria. Each of the daughters divides again, and so on and so on. Sometimes, mutations occur when the bacteria divides, as in any other DNA replication process. In time, these mutations cause the bacteria to change and evolve.

Scientists are working on new definitions for species that work for all types of organisms. Scientists who study bacteria have found that they can group them into different categories. For example, some bacteria are found in the gut, while others cause staph infections. Scientists have given these separate, recognizable categories of bacteria names and call them a species.

WHEN ONE BECOMES TWO

Some members of a species branch off and become a separate species. This process is called speciation, and it takes many, many hundreds of years. Speciation happens when two different populations of the same species evolve in different ways. While they start off the same, the two populations become more and more different with time. Eventually, they are so different, they are no longer able to **interbreed**.

Speciation takes a very long time. Scientists can't watch speciation happen in a lab. Instead, they observe speciation in nature and study the individual parts of the process.

Imagine that you are studying fruit flies. You notice that there are different species of fruit flies. How could that happen? In one possible scenario, one population of fruit flies buzzes around an island, laying their eggs in bananas. Then a hurricane passes over the island, and some of the bananas and immature fruit flies are washed out to sea! Eventually, these bananas and fruit flies land on a different island. When the fruit flies mature, they emerge into this new land. The fruit flies on the first island are too far away to breed with the fruit flies on the second island.

However, speciation still has not occurred. If you transported any of the fruit flies on the second island back to the first island, they would be able to interbreed and produce fertile offspring with the first group of fruit flies.

The conditions on the two islands are different. Because of the different conditions, the fruit flies in each location evolve under different natural selection pressures and experience different random events.

After many, many generations, each group shows changes in form, food preferences, and mating rituals. Natural selection is causing changes in the species.

One day, a traveler brings a bunch of bananas from the second island back to the first island. Eggs from the second group of fruit flies travel with the bananas. The second group of fruit flies is no longer able to easily mate with the first group. They have evolved to follow different mating rituals.

DID YOU KNOW? An incipient species is a group of organisms that is about to become a separate species from another.

If they are able to mate, their offspring will not be **viable** because of genetic differences that now exist between the two groups. Genes can no longer flow between the two populations. Speciation has occurred.

WORDS TO KNOW

reproductive isolation: when two populations lose their ability to produce live or fertile offspring.

migrate: when an organism moves from one location to another.

habitat: the natural home or environment surrounding an organism.

geographic isolation: when changing geography creates physical barriers between populations.

allopatric speciation: the development of a new species due to a geographic barrier.

WHY DOES SPECIATION HAPPEN?

Speciation doesn't just happen overnight. It takes a lot of time! And it usually involves three components: a reduction in gene flow, a decrease in the genetic similarities among populations, and **reproductive isolation**.

When organisms in a species mate and reproduce, that keeps the genes between populations mixed. As long as the genes can easily flow between populations, the two populations remain basically the same genetically. They have the same gene frequencies. For example, if one out of ten individuals has genes for red hair in one population, the other populations will also have one out of ten individuals with red hair.

Sometimes, something happens to slow or even stop the flow of genes between two populations. Changes in geography can create physical barriers between populations. Rivers change direction, mountains rise, continents drift apart, and organisms **migrate** to new **habitats**, such as the fruit flies we discussed earlier. All of these changes create something called **geographic isolation**, which can divide a larger single population into two or more smaller populations.

Sometimes, geographic isolation occurs even without a physical barrier. An unfavorable habitat between two populations can keep them from mating with each other. Among most groups of organisms, geographic isolation is the most common cause of speciation. This is also called **allopatric speciation**.

Snapping shrimp are one example of allopatric speciation. Approximately 3 million years ago, the Isthmus of Panama closed, which meant the snapping shrimp were separated into two populations with a land barrier between them. Although the shrimp looked similar, when scientists put them together, they refused to mate. The two shrimp populations had evolved differently for 3 million years. They had become separate species!

Sometimes, a reduction in gene flow occurs even without a geographic barrier that prevents mating between two populations. Organisms tend to mate with others that are nearby. When a population lives across a large geographic area, organisms at one end of the area are very unlikely to mate with organisms at the other end of the area—they'll find a closer mate, because it's easier. So, although each section of the population is not isolated, gene flow is definitely reduced.

DID YOU KNOW?

For allopatric speciation, gene flow between two populations must be greatly reduced, but it doesn't have to be reduced completely to zero. It can still occur even if a few individuals can cross the barrier to mate with members of the other group.

In some cases, the reduction in gene flow is enough to cause speciation to begin. If the organisms at the opposite ends of the area experience different evolutionary forces, the gene frequencies in each group might change so much over time that the two groups would not be able to mate if they were brought together.

SYMPATRIC SPECIATION

sympatric speciation: the process through which new species evolve from a single species while living in the same geographic region.

parapatric speciation: evolution of a new species because of an extreme change in habitat.

WORDS TO KNOW

SYMPATRIC SPECIATION

Another type of speciation occurs when something in the environment reduces the gene flow between two populations. **Sympatric speciation** occurs without the organisms in two populations being physically separated. For example, one combination of genes might allow some individuals to find food more easily at night, while another gene combination makes other individuals better at finding food during the day. If some individuals are only active at night, while others are only active during the day, it is unlikely that they will breed with each other. And that will cause a reduction in the gene flow between the groups.

Scientists believe that although sympatric speciation is not common, it can be an important process.

The apple maggot worm is a good example of sympatric speciation. Apples were brought to the United States by European settlers. Native to the United States, the apple maggot worm fed on hawthorn fruit before apples arrived in America. Today, some apple maggot worms feed on apples, while others still feed on hawthorns. Because hawthorns and apples can grow in similar locations, the adult flies of the worms that infest apple trees have the opportunity to mate with the adult flies of the worms from hawthorns.

Apple maggot fly (Joseph Berger, Bugwood.org)

Yet, when scientists examine the worms, the two groups are genetically different. Something is blocking the gene flow between the two groups. The flies that lay eggs on apples are avoiding laying eggs on hawthorns. Scientists believe that one factor is that apples ripen earlier than hawthorn fruit. This might have led the flies living on each plant type to evolve to reproduce at different times.

In addition, the flies seem to have developed a feeding preference for either apples or hawthorns. This feeding preference is another factor that reduces gene flow. At this point, the two populations of apple maggot flies can still mate and reproduce. Speciation has not yet occurred, but it might be in the early stages.

Parapatric Speciation

Sometimes, speciation occurs even when there is no geographic barrier. In **parapatric speciation**, the two populations are not physically separated. Instead, they live next to each other. They are within mating distance, but something else causes them to stick to their side, reducing the gene flow between them. Generally, that barrier is natural selection. Parapatric speciation is extremely rare.

Scientists believe that the grass species *Anthoxanthum odoratum* might be experiencing the first steps of parapatric speciation. Some of these grass plants live near mines in soil contaminated with heavy metals. While the plants haven't speciated yet, natural selection has favored plants that are able to survive in soil with high concentrations of heavy metals. At the same time, other plants of the same species live nearby in uncontaminated soil. The metal-tolerant and metal-intolerant plants are geographically close enough that they could fertilize each other, but the offspring are not likely to survive because each side has different selective pressures. With time, the genetic change between the two populations will only increase. They could eventually become two separate species.

Anthoxanthum odoratum

(Christiaan Sepp, 1807)

BARRIERS

What prevents separate species from producing offspring? There are two main types of barriers: **prezygotic barriers** and **postzygotic barriers**. Prezygotic barriers prevent mating from ever happening. A prezygotic barrier can be different mating rituals, different mating seasons, different niches within a habitat, and more.

For example, the blue-footed booby bird has a complex mating ritual. Although there are several other, closely related bird species living in the same area, the female blue-footed booby will mate only with males that follow a specific mating ritual.

Other times, two species have different mating seasons. For example, while the American toad and Fowler's toad can mate in a laboratory, they do not mate in nature, because the Fowler's toad has a later mating season than the American toad. Some species may not mate when they live in different parts of the same habitat because they do not come in contact with each other.

MATING SEASON

AMERICAN TOAD   FOWLER'S TOAD

Postzygotic barriers occur after the species have mated. Sometimes, a viable offspring does not form. Other times, the mating produces an offspring, but it is unable to reproduce. Remember the example of the mule? A horse and a donkey can mate and create a mule offspring. However, the mule is **sterile**.

Behavioral Isolation

Behavioral isolation is one type of reproductive barrier. It is based on an organism's behavior—usually, its mating rituals and signals. Signals that attract individuals to each other are a critical part of successful mating. In nature, there are many examples of behavioral isolation. Have you watched fireflies flashing on a summer's evening? The males of certain firefly species attract females by flashing their lights in specific patterns. The females are attracted only to the flashing patterns by the males in their own species. This behavior prevents them from mating with fireflies from other, closely related species. Other species follow specific mating rituals, songs, or vocalizations to attract the opposite sex. These behaviors prevent them from mating with others that do not show these behaviors. Can you imagine a world in which every birdsong was the same?

REPRODUCTIVE ISOLATION

Geographic isolation might start the process of speciation by putting up external barriers to gene flow, but that is not enough to create two separate species. For speciation to be complete, genetic changes must occur to finish the process. Internal, or genetically based, barriers to gene flow are needed. If internal barriers do not develop, individuals from two populations will be able to interbreed when they get together again. Their genes will mix again and any genetic differences that had developed between the two will eventually disappear.

For speciation to occur, the two species must avoid mating with each other and be unable to produce viable offspring together. This is called reproductive isolation, when two separate populations lose their ability to produce live or fertile offspring.

Internal barriers to gene flow include anything that prevents sperm and egg from coming together. The two populations might have evolved to have different mating locations, mating times, or mating rituals. These differences could make it almost impossible for two individuals to get together to mate. Other times, sexual organs could have evolved so they no longer fit together. For some insects, this can prevent mating and complete speciation.

Even if individuals from the two populations are able to mate, if their offspring does not survive or cannot reproduce, speciation is complete. Sometimes, the offspring are never born, while other times they die young before reproducing.

In the fruit fly example, geographic isolation triggered the process of speciation. The two fruit fly populations lived on different islands and experienced different natural selection pressures that caused the second population to change genetically. Perhaps the second island grew more pineapples than bananas. The fruit flies on that island evolved to prefer the abundant pineapple. When these flies returned to the first island, they continued to hang out near pineapples. If fruit flies find their mates near a food source, the pineapple flies would not mix with the banana flies. Gene flow would be significantly reduced. More genetic differences between the two groups of fruit flies could develop.

COSPECIATION

Sometimes, two species are very closely associated. So close, in fact, that if one speciates, the other might speciate at the same time. This process is called cospeciation. Often, cospeciation occurs with parasites and their hosts. To understand cospeciation in practice, think about a species of louse living on a rodent. When the rodents come together to mate, the lice can switch hosts. They can mate with lice on the other rodent. This allows genes to flow through the louse species.

Now, imagine what would happen if a flood cut off one population of the rodents from the others. The rodents would not be able to mate with the other populations. Gene flow between the populations would be greatly reduced. The rodents could become reproductively isolated. Genetic changes from natural selection forces might lead to speciation for the rodents.

For the lice, the flood also causes geographic isolation. Because the rodents are no longer mingling and mating with the other group, the lice no longer have the opportunity to switch hosts and mate with other lice. The louse population's gene flow is also greatly reduced. It also might become speciated.

Speciation is an amazing process that makes our world a diverse one. How do scientists keep track of all of the different species and their ancestors? In the next chapter, we'll learn how to trace evolution in a coherent way to better understand how it works.

? ESSENTIAL QUESTION

Now it's time to consider and discuss the Essential Question: Why are there different paths to speciation? Why is speciation important to continued life on Earth?

Stranded on a Desert Island

What would happen if you and your classmates were stranded on a desert island? In this activity, you will explore the process of developing a new species.

❯ **Imagine that you and a small group** of classmates are stranded on a desert island. The island's climate is **tropical**. Its average temperature is 80 degrees Fahrenheit (27 degrees Celsius) and only varies by plus or minus 20 degrees. There are intermittent heavy rainstorms nearly every day. Lush foliage grows throughout the island. Fish and fruit are plentiful food sources.

❯ **A second group of classmates** is stranded on a different island. Their island is covered in snow for 10 months of the year. Temperatures rarely rise above 10 degrees Fahrenheit (-12 degrees Celsius) in the winter. In the winter, there are only two to four hours of daylight, while summer months have about 20 hours of daylight. Summer temperatures are in the 50s. They can hunt a small number of Arctic foxes and penguin-like birds. The most plentiful food source is fish. Fruits and vegetables are only available during the short summer season.

❯ **Have each group consider** the following questions.

★ What traits do you and the people in your group have that would help you survive on this island?

★ After 500 generations, describe what your group's **descendants** are like. Don't forget that each generation should have gotten better at surviving on the island. What do they look like? What senses do they use the most?

❯ **During the next 500 generations,** many small mutations occur. List 10 visible mutations that would improve survival on the island.

★ What does a descendant on the island look like after 1,000 generations or more? How did mutations and natural selection affect this most recent generation? Draw a picture to illustrate this individual.

❯ **After 1,000 generations,** compare each island's population.

★ How are they similar? How are they different?

WORDS TO KNOW

tropical: the hot climate zone to the north and south of the equator.

descendant: a person related to someone who lived in the past.

	Tropical Island	Cold Island
Traits after 500 generations		
Traits after 1,000 generations		

* Do you think the two populations are genetically different from each other? Why or why not?

* Do you think either population has become a new species? Explain your answer.

TRY THIS: Consider the population on a third island with desert conditions. How do the descendants of this island compare to the others in this activity.

Diane Dodd's Fruit Fly Experiments

A scientist named Diane Dodd studied the effects of geographic isolation and natural selection on fruit flies. She took fruit flies from one population and placed them into different cages to simulate geographic isolation. Some of the caged populations lived on sugar-based food. The other populations lived on starch-based foods. After many generations, researchers tested the flies to see which flies they preferred for mating. They found that the sugar flies preferred other sugar flies, while starch flies preferred other starch flies. Scientists suspect that these mating preferences evolved because natural selection for food sources also affected genes related to reproductive behavior. In other words, the genes that helped flies survive better on sugar foods also affected their mating preferences. The results suggest that geographic isolation can lead to the beginning of reproductive isolation.

All-y-oop Speciation

Allopatric speciation occurs when a physical barrier separates
two populations of a species. Because genes cannot flow
between the two groups, the process of speciation can begin.
After much time, speciation might lead to two distinct species.
In this activity, you'll make a model of allopatric speciation.

❯ **To begin, you'll need beads,** candies, or other small objects in two
different colors. Put equal numbers of each color bead (Color A and Color
B) into a large bowl or plastic cup. These represent alleles that could be
inherited from a mother. Also put equal numbers of each color bead into
another bowl or cup. This represents alleles inherited from a father.

❯ **Create offspring by taking one bead** from the mother cup and one
from the father cup and putting them into a smaller paper cup. Try to pick
the beads randomly. Spread the offspring cups across a table to represent a
geographic area.

❯ **Examine the offspring cups** across the table. Are there any areas with
a concentration of Color A? What about Color B? Create a geographic barrier
on the tabletop to separate the concentration of same-colored beads from
the rest of the population. The population with a concentration of one color
is now permanently separated from the other population and can no longer
mate with it.

❯ **Count Color A and Color B** in each population. What are each
population's gene frequencies? How does this differ from the original
population's gene frequencies?

❯ **Assign a trait to Color A and Color B genes.** How is this shown in the
two populations? Through time, if there is no gene flow between the two
populations, what do you predict will happen? Explain why.

TRY THIS: What would happen to the two populations if they experienced the
same environmental conditions and natural selection pressures? Explain your
thoughts.

Is It a Species?

Sometimes, different animals can get together to produce some pretty interesting offspring. Sometimes, these offspring are a new species. Other times, they are not. In some cases, the answer is not entirely clear. In this activity, you'll take a look at a few of these combinations and determine if you think the offspring is a new species.

❯ Example #1 – A Liger and a Tigon

In nature, lions and tigers do not mate because they generally live in different habitats. In captivity, these two animals are able to produce offspring. When a female tiger and a male lion mate, their offspring is called a liger. The offspring of a male tiger and a female lion is called a tigon. Male ligers are not able to produce offspring, but female ligers can produce offspring with either tigers or lions. Do you think the liger is a separate species from the lion and tiger? Explain.

❯ Example #2 – Goldendoodles

Many dog breeds can mate with each other to produce offspring. Their offspring have a combination of the parents' traits. For example, Golden Retrievers and poodles can be bred to produce Goldendoodles. This mixed-breed dog is healthy and able to reproduce with other dogs. Do you think the Goldendoodle is a separate species? Explain.

TRY THIS: What about bacteria? *Escherichia coli* (*E. coli*) bacteria is typically found in the human gut. Most of the time, it is harmless and may even help digestion. However,

(William Warby)

there is a strain of *E. coli* bacteria that produces a toxin that can kill a person. Under the microscope, the two strains of *E. coli* look very similar. When comparing their genomes, the toxic strain is missing 528 genes that the harmless strain has. The toxic strain also has more than 1,300 genes not found in the harmless strain. Do you think these two bacteria are separate species? Explain.

African Indigobirds

Sometimes, speciation occurs because of behavioral barriers. Two populations live in the same geographic area, but certain behaviors reduce gene flow between them. In this activity, you'll explore the example of the African indigobirds.

❯ **Read the following description** of African indigobird populations and decide if they are separate species.

When African indigobirds lay their eggs, they lay them in the nests of different species of finches. The blue indigobird lays eggs in both the African firefinch and black-bellied firefinch nests. When the eggs hatch, the newborn indigobirds learn the songs of the finches they are with. As adults, the indigobirds use the songs of the finches in their own mating songs. Although the two populations of indigobirds can still mate and produce fertile offspring, female indigobirds prefer to mate with males that know the same finch songs. A female indigobird that hatched in a black-bellied firefinch nest prefers to mate with a male who hatched in the same type of nest. In addition, the female tends to lay her eggs in the black-bellied firefinch nest instead of the nest of an African firefinch.

✱ Do you think the two indigobird populations are separate species?

✱ Why or why not?

CONSIDER THIS: What do you predict will happen to these two populations in the future? Explain your answer.

The Founder Effect

The founder effect occurs when a small number of individuals colonizes a new area. Because the new colony has a small population, it might have less genetic variation than the larger, original population. It could also have a higher percentage of certain genes as compared to the original population. In these conditions, the genes of the founders are more likely to be passed down to offspring. If the founders carry an unusually high frequency of a gene for a particular disease, the new population will also have an unusually high frequency of that gene.

Chapter 3

CLASSIFICATION
AND THE TREE OF LIFE

Through speciation, one species can evolve into two separate species. Then, two becomes four, and four becomes eight, again and again. Throughout Earth's long history, the process of evolution has created the diversity of life all around you. Today, scientists believe there are about 8.7 million species on Earth! And all of it is possible through evolution.

Life has a history. It certainly hasn't stayed the same since its very beginnings! Species that are different today might have had common ancestors in the past. Change and speciation have created the tree of life.

WORDS TO KNOW

lineage: a continuous line of descent connecting ancestors and descendants.

evolutionary tree: a tree-like diagram that shows evolutionary relationships.

diverge: to separate from the main path and go in another direction.

phylogenetic: based on evolutionary relationships.

mnemonic: a tool, pattern, or association used to help remember something.

ESSENTIAL QUESTION

Why is the structure of a tree useful for scientists who are classifying organisms according to common ancestors?

Have you ever made a family tree? Your family tree allows you to trace your family history and see all of your ancestors and family relationships. In a similar way, evolution has created a pattern of relationships between species. Some species share a direct **lineage**. Others are closely related cousins. Just as people create family trees, scientists create **evolutionary trees** to show the family history and relationships for a particular set of species. As species evolve and split into two, their evolutionary paths **diverge** and create new branches on the evolutionary tree. Evolutionary trees are also called **phylogenetic** trees.

DID YOU KNOW?

Taxonomy is the science of naming, describing, and classifying organisms.

LINNAEAN VS. PHYLOGENETIC CLASSIFICATION

Most scientists like to classify things. They like to group similar items together. When they do this, they can often learn more about each item. Simply sorting items can reveal patterns and relationships between them. It can also give clues about past events, information that is critical to the study of evolution. Two systems of classification that biologists use are Linnaean classification and phylogenetic classification.

In the 1700s, Swedish botanist Carolus Linnaeus (1707-1778) developed a way to name and organize species. He divided every organism into two kingdoms: animal and vegetable. Then he subdivided those kingdoms into classes, which were further divided into smaller and smaller subgroups.

Using this system of classification, every organism is assigned to a kingdom, phylum, class, order, family, genus, and species. Today, scientists have modified the Linnaean classification system to include new discoveries and knowledge. They think there are at least six kingdoms—animals, plants, fungi, archaebacteria, eubacteria, and protists.

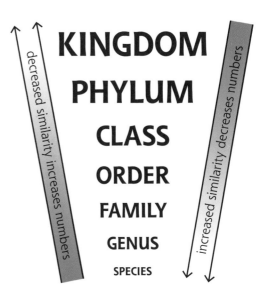

KINGDOM
PHYLUM
CLASS
ORDER
FAMILY
GENUS
SPECIES

decreased similarity increases numbers

increased similarity decreases numbers

A handy way to memorize the Linnaean system of classification is to use this **mnemonic:**
<u>K</u>ing <u>P</u>hilip <u>C</u>ame <u>O</u>ver <u>F</u>or <u>G</u>ood <u>S</u>oup.

Linnaeus created his classification system before scientists understood that organisms evolved. Because his system is not based on evolution, many biologists also use a classification system that incorporates an organism's evolutionary history.

Let's look at the example of a red-winged blackbird, a bird found in many parts of North and Central America. It's Latin name is *A. phoeniceus*. What does a diagram of its evolutionary tree look like? What about a phylogenetic classification of birds to explore more about the lineage of a red-winged blackbird?

Evolutionary tree of red-winged blackbird	
Kingdom	*Animalia*
Phylum	*Chordata*
Class	*Aves*
Order	*Passeriformes*
Family	*Icteridae*
Genus	*Agelaius*
Species	A. phoeniceus

clade: a group of organisms descended from a common ancestor.

ectothermic: cold-blooded. Describes animals such as snakes that have a body temperature that varies with the surrounding temperature.

reptile: a cold-blooded animal such as a snake, lizard, alligator, or turtle, that has a spine, lays eggs, has scales or horny places, and breathes air.

pathogen: a bacteria, virus, or other microorganism that can cause disease.

immune system: the system of cells that protects your body against disease and infection. Includes white blood cells.

cladogram: a type of evolutionary tree.

A phylogenetic classification system puts organisms into categories called **clades**, which are groups of organisms that are descended from a common ancestor. As in the Linnaean system, the clades are nested so that an organism is assigned a series of groups that locates it more and more specifically within the system.

For example, a Linnaean classification might place birds and non-avian dinosaurs into two separate groups. However, the evolutionary history of these two groups shows that the bird lineage branched off the dinosaur lineage. So, according to a phylogenetic classification, birds are part of the group Dinosauria. Our red-winged blackbird is distantly related to dinosaurs!

To switch from a Linnaean system of classification to a phylogenetic system, scientists reassign names to clades. In many cases, the Linnaean system's names work well in the phylogenetic system. For

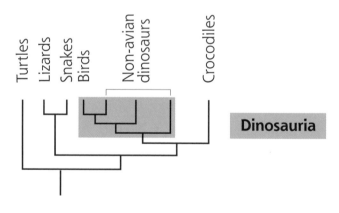

example, Aves is a class of birds in the Linnaean system. It is also a clade and uses the same name in a phylogenetic system.

Other times, there are some differences. For example, in the Linnaean system, the class reptilian contains all animals that are **ectothermic** and have scales. Birds are not classified as **reptiles**. But in a phylogenetic system, reptiles do not form their own clade. Instead, reptiles are included in a clade with birds because they share a common ancestor.

Through phylogenetic classification, scientists have been able to trace the genetic history of different species. They have found evidence that supports that the processes of speciation have occurred. In fact, they have gathered evidence that all life descends from a single common ancestor. For example, the fact that all organisms have a very similar form of DNA, the instruction manual for life, is one piece of evidence for a common ancestor.

DID YOU KNOW?
Some scientists believe that viruses should have their own kingdom in the Linnaean classification system.

Phylogenetic classifications also allow scientists to better predict the future.

Understanding the history of species and how they changed with time can help scientists anticipate future changes and mutations. In health care, scientists are using information learned from phylogenetics to predict the behavior and mutation of viruses and other disease-causing **pathogens** that attack the human **immune system**.

EVOLUTIONARY TREES

Biologists use evolutionary trees such as **cladograms** and phylogenetic trees to visually show the evolutionary relationships among organisms. Evolutionary trees group related organisms in clades. If the grouping does not include all of an ancestor's descendants, it is not a clade. If the grouping does not include a common ancestor, it is not a clade.

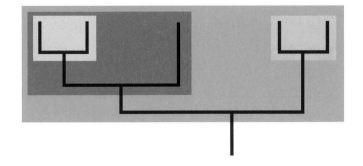

Some clades are small and include only a few species. Other clades are very large, including thousands of species. A clade can even be nested within a larger clade. In the diagram above, each colored rectangle shows a clade.

Each branch on the tree represents a speciation event, when one species evolved into another. The base of the tree represents the ancestor, while the tips of the branches represent the ancestor's descendants. Moving from the tree's roots to branch tips, you move forward in time.

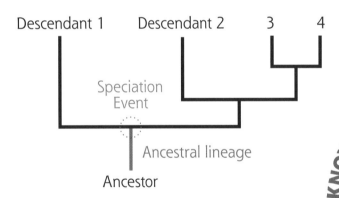

A phylogenetic tree has branches and nodes where branches connect. When speciation occurs, it creates a new branch on the tree. The point or node where the ancestral lineage splits into two branches is when the speciation event occurred.

DID YOU KNOW?

Why do biologists use two systems of classification? Both are useful. The phylogenetic system is useful for understanding the relationships between animals, while the Linnaean system is more useful for understanding how animals live.

Looking at a phylogenetic tree, you can trace a species' ancestors and see related species.

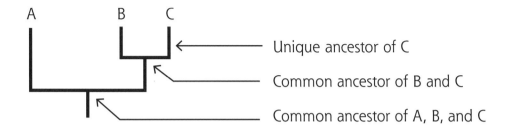

Sometimes, a clade looks like a pitchfork. This is called a **polytomy**, a node that has more than two descendent lineages. Sometimes, this happens when scientists do not yet have enough data to determine how lineages in the pitchfork are related. Other times, multiple speciation occurred at the same time, creating a polytomy. When this happens, all of the descendant lineages are equally closely related to each other.

What's the Difference?

When talking about evolution and evolutionary relationships, many scientists use several terms almost interchangeably—phylogeny, evolutionary tree, phylogenetic tree, and cladogram. All of these terms can be used for a tree structure that visually represents the evolutionary relationships among a group of organisms. However, some scientists use these terms with subtle differences. For example, some scientists use the term "cladogram" when talking about a diagram that represents a hypothesis about the group's actual evolutionary history. In addition, the lengths of branches don't matter in a cladogram. The branches are not used to represent the amount of time it took for evolutionary change to occur. In a phylogeny, species are still grouped by similarities and physical or genetic traits. The branch lengths represent the relative time it took for evolutionary changes to occur. A phylogenetic tree also shows how ancestors are related to their descendants and how those descendants have changed through time.

HOW SCIENTISTS BUILD A TREE

When you make your family tree, you probably have information and papers that show who your ancestors were and what their relationships are to you and each other. In nature, species do not have paperwork to show their ancestors and family relationships. Instead, scientists must collect and analyze evidence to construct their histories. With this evidence, scientists form a hypothesis about how the species are related, or the phylogeny.

Phylogenetic trees visually represent patterns of relationships among species and their lineages.

To build a phylogenetic tree, scientists collect data about the organisms they wish to study. They search for clues about the relationships between different species. Then, they analyze the information to come up with a hypothesis about the tree. They identify **characters** of each organism, or heritable traits that can be compared across organisms, such as physical characteristics, genetic sequences, and behavioral traits.

DID YOU KNOW?

Many phylogenetic trees also include an **outgroup**, which is an organism outside the group being studied. The outgroup is not as closely related to the members of the group. Looking at an outgroup can give scientists a better idea of where the group of organisms falls on the bigger tree of life.

To begin building a tree, scientists choose the organisms they want to study. They identify the organism's specific, measurable traits, or characteristics. What color eyes does the organism have? Does it have hair or a bony skeleton? How many limbs does it have? These are a few examples of characteristics that form characters. When studying characters, scientists also look for clues about which character state came first. Did all of the organisms have four limbs and then did some evolve to have only two limbs?

Knowing which character came first helps scientists understand how evolution happens through time.

Next, scientists want to see what the species have in common. A shared character is one that both species have, such as the ability to lay eggs. A **derived character** is one that evolved in a clade's ancestral history. The members of the clade have that character, but others outside the clade do not. Using the shared derived characters, scientists can group organisms into clades. For example, **amphibians**, turtles, lizards, snakes, crocodiles, birds, and **mammals** have all had four limbs at one point in their histories. Four limbs is a shared derived character for these animals. This character was inherited from a common ancestor. And it is what makes this group of animals different compared to other organisms.

HOMOLOGOUS CHARACTERS

When comparing character states among different species, you have to make sure that you're looking at different states of the same character instead of two different characters. **Homologous characters** are characters in different organisms that are similar and were inherited from a common ancestor.

One example of a homologous character is the presence of forelimbs. Humans have forelimbs, while earthworms do not. Because forelimbs in **vertebrates** share a common ancestor, they are homologous. Even though they are homologous, they can evolve in different ways. Forelimbs have evolved into wings in birds, flippers in dolphins, arms in humans, and front legs in dogs.

Not all characters that appear similar are homologous. For example, both birds and bats have wings. Does that mean that birds and bats are closely related to each other? Not necessarily. When you look closely at bird and bat wings, there are some big differences. A bird's wings are made of feathers that stretch along the arm. A bat's wings are made from flaps of skin stretched across the fingers and arm bones.

The differences in wing structure are clues that bats and birds did not inherit their wings from the same ancestor.

DID YOU KNOW?

Although birds and bats did not inherit wings from a common ancestor with wings, they did inherit forelimbs from a common ancestor with forelimbs. Therefore, while they are analogous as wings, they are homologous as forelimbs.

Because they have separate evolutionary origins, bat and bird wings are **analogous**. They might appear to be similar—after all, they are both wings—because natural selection has shaped them to perform best in flight. This often happens when both lineages live in similar environments and experience similar selective pressures.

Evolution occurs during a long period of time. Evolutionary changes have occurred at different points in time, often in between long periods of little change. On a phylogenetic tree, scientists show time in the lengths of the branches. Each branch length is drawn in **proportion** to the amount of time that passed between when lineages arose and split.

How do we know everything that we know about evolution? How do we find the information we need to create these evolutionary trees? In the next chapter, we'll take a look at some of the ways scientists make their discoveries and where they find evidence of evolution.

ESSENTIAL QUESTION

Now it's time to consider and discuss the Essential Question: Why is the structure of a tree useful for scientists who are classifying organisms according to common ancestors?

Fins – Homologous or Analogous?

Fish have fins. So do penguins. In both species, fins help the animals navigate and move through water. So does that make fish and penguins closely related? Are fins homologous characters? Actually, because a penguin is a bird and a fish is not, it is pretty clear that these two species are not closely related. They did not inherit their fins from the same ancestor. Instead, fins are analogous characters for fish and penguins. They evolved in both species because they were a functional feature that helped the animals survive in their aquatic environments.

Make Your Own Cladogram

Cladograms can be difficult to make. Knowing how to construct a cladogram can help you understand evolutionary relationships.

❯ **Start by picking four to six animals** to be in your cladogram. They should all be from the same order or family, according to the Linnaean classification system. You can also select another animal outside of this group to be part of your outgroup. An outgroup is something to compare against the other organisms in the cladogram.

❯ **Take an inventory** of the characteristics of the species you are going to compare. Create a characteristic chart.

❯ **What do all of the animals you picked**, including the animal in the outgroup, have in common? This is the ancestral characteristic. It links the animal in the outgroup to the other animals. For example, if you chose a tuna, salamander, turtle, and leopard, they could all share the trait of having a jaw.

❯ **Next, determine what makes your animals different** from each other. In this example, the salamander, turtle, and leopard all have four legs, while the tuna does not. This makes the tuna part of the outgroup.

❯ **Looking at the in-group animals,** what characteristics make them different from each other? In our example, turtles and leopards have an amniotic egg, which separates them from salamanders. Then, what characteristic separates turtles and leopards? Hair!

DID YOU KNOW?

An amniotic egg is the type of egg produced by reptiles, birds, and mammals. The fluid-filled egg is either laid on land or kept inside the animal while the baby develops.

❭ **Using this information, make a list** of the derived characteristics for each animal in your in-group, from the most ancestral to the most derived. In the example, the ancestral characteristic of jaws groups the tuna, salamander, turtle, and leopard together. The derived character of having four legs groups the salamander, turtle, and leopard together.

❭ **Next draw your cladogram.** Place the animal in the outgroup at the first line on the left as shown here.

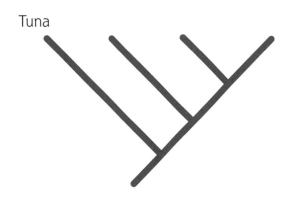

❭ **Place the least derived animal** in the in-group on the line next to the outgroup.

❭ **Continue filling in each line,** with the most derived animal placed at the end of the diagonal line. You can also write the derived characteristics on the cladogram.

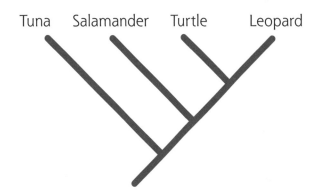

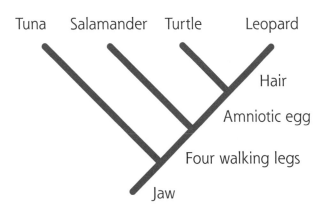

CONSIDER THIS: How could you turn this cladogram into a phylogenetic tree? What element does a phylogenic tree have that a cladogram does not?

Read a Cladogram

A cladogram is a type of evolutionary tree. It provides a lot of information about different species and their relationships. Study the cladogram below. Then show what you know by answering the questions underneath.

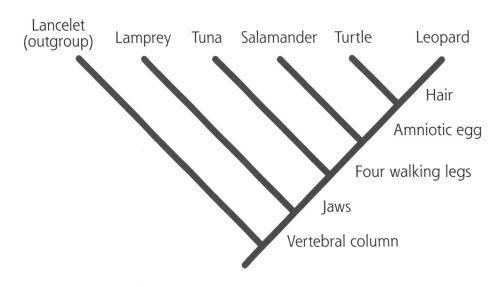

❯ Looking at this cladogram, consider the following.

✱ What trait separates lamprey from tuna, salamanders, turtles, and leopards?

✱ What separates turtles and leopards from salamanders?

✱ Which organism is most related to the leopard?

✱ What four traits do these two organisms share?

✱ Which organism will have DNA most similar to the leopard?

✱ Which organism's DNA will be the most different from the leopard?

TRY THIS: Find two clades on this cladogram. What organisms are included in the clade? Explain why it is a clade.

Design a Classification System

Scientists classify objects through grouping them by common characteristics. Classification makes objects easier to find, identify, and study. Throughout history, scientists have developed methods to classify animals and plants according to certain physical similarities. In the Linnaean classification system, classification starts with broad groupings. Then, the next level of classification gets more specific, eliminating organisms that could be in the previous level. In this activity, you will design your own classification system for objects in your classroom or home.

❯ **Use the Linnaean system** as a model to create your own classification system for everyday objects in your house or classroom.

❯ **Start with a classification level** that divides objects into a few main categories. The categories in the first classification level should combine to include all objects in the house. Then create at least four subsequent levels of classification, each of which becomes more specific.

❯ **Share your classification system** with your classmates, friends, and family. Do they agree with how you classified objects?

TRY THIS: Think about how we classify objects in everyday life. How do you use classification to organize your desk, room, or closet? How does classification make your life easier?

Scientific Names

Every species on Earth has a two-part scientific name. This allows people all around the world to communicate easily about a specific species, without getting confused by common nicknames. Scientists use a formal naming system to assign scientific names to a species. For example, you might call your dog "Lily," but her scientific name is *Canis familiaris*. The first part of a scientific name is its genus from the Linnaean classification system. A genus is a small group of closely related organisms. The second part of a scientific name, the specific epithet, is used to identify a particular species as separate from other species in the same genus. Together, these two parts make the scientific name. When writing a scientific name, both names should be italicized. Also, the genus name always starts with a capital letter and the specific epithet always starts with a lowercase letter.

Use Linnaeus's Classification System

Linnaeus's system classifies plants and animals on seven levels. For example, the brown squirrel is classified as follows.

Level	Classification	Meaning
Kingdom	Animalia	animal
Phylum	Chordata	With a backbone
Class	Mammalia	Has a backbone and nurses its young
Order	Rodentia	Has a backbone, nurses its young, and has long, sharp front teeth
Family	Scuridae	Has a backbone, nurses its young, has long, sharp front teeth, and has a bushy tail
Genus	Tamiasciurus	Has a backbone, nurses its young, has long, sharp front teeth, has a bushy tail, and climbs trees
Species	hudsonicus	Has a backbone, nurses its young, has long, sharp front teeth, has a bushy tail, climbs trees, and has brown fur on the back and white fur underneath

Each level gets more specific, excluding organisms that may have been included in the prior level. For example, horses are also part of the same kingdom, phylum, and class as the brown squirrel. However, horses are excluded from the order Rodentia because they do not have long, sharp front teeth. Often, scientists don't go through the entire seven-level classification system to identify plants and animals. Instead, they shorten it to just the genus and species. The scientific name of the brown squirrel is *Tamiasciurus hudsonicus*.

> **Using the Internet with permission or a biology book,** find the genus and species names of the following animals and plants.

* Dogs
* Cats
* Horses
* Pigs
* Oak trees
* Evergreen trees

TRY THIS: Now, go back and find other organisms that share the same genus but are different species. How are the two organisms alike? What makes them different?

Design a Dichotomous Key

In biology, classification of organisms is very important. As we learn more about species and discover new species, it is important to have a system to identify and classify organisms. A **dichotomous key** is a tool that helps to identify unknown organisms. It uses a series of statements that are made up of two choices that describe the unknown organism's characteristics. For example, the statement might read "The flower is red" or "The flower is blue." The key user chooses which of the two statements best describes the unknown organism. Then, they follow the path to the next set of statements and answer those. Eventually, the statements lead to the identity of the unknown organism. Dichotomous keys are frequently used in field guides to help identify plants and animals. In this activity, you will learn how to create and use a dichotomous key.

❯ **To begin, take a look online** to study examples of dichotomous keys. You can find examples here.

dichotomous key leaves 🔍

dichotomous key pine trees 🔍

❯ **Begin by making a dichotomous key** to identify your classmates. Start with general statements and get more specific with each following statement. You can organize your key as a series of questions, a flow chart, or other format you prefer.

❯ **Once you've finished the key,** give it to a classmate to test. Do they get the expected result?

❯ **Once you are comfortable with the process** of creating and using a dichotomous key, design one to identify organisms in nature. These can be animals, plants, insects, or other organisms. Once you've finished, test the key. Does it identify the organisms correctly?

TRY THIS: Create a new dichotomous key to identify a local species of tree, plant, or insect. Take a walk in your neighborhood with your key and identify the organisms you see.

WORDS TO KNOW

dichotomous key: a key to classification based on a choice between two alternative characters.

59

Chapter 4

EVIDENCE
FOR EVOLUTION

The central idea of evolution is that life has existed on Earth for billions of years and has changed during this time. While scientists debate the details, they agree that an overwhelming amount of evidence supports the theory of evolution. But how is the history of life on Earth documented?

Do you have photo books and videos of your family through the years? We have no pictures or videos of life from millions of years ago, because cameras (and people to work them) weren't around yet. Instead, scientists study evidence in nature to reconstruct the history of life on Earth.

Some types of evidence include **fossils** and similarities between living organisms. These were used by Darwin and are still used by scientists today. Modern scientists have also taken advantage of advances in technology to use other types of evidence, such as DNA testing, to learn more about evolution.

fossil: the preserved remains of a dead organism or the remains of an organism's actions.

paleontologist: a scientist who studies fossils and the creatures that made them.

mammoth: a large extinct mammal that was hairy with a sloping back and long, curved tusks.

fossil record: all fossils taken together.

WORDS TO KNOW

FOSSIL EVIDENCE

? ESSENTIAL QUESTION

How do scientists learn about time periods that happened before written history?

Fossils are pictures of the past that help tell the history of how life has happened for billions of years. A fossil can be the preserved remains of a dead organism. It can also be the remains of an organism's actions, such as footprints or burrows. Sometimes, **paleontologists** find an animal's or plant's entire fossilized body, such as a **mammoth** encased in ice or an insect trapped in amber.

DID YOU KNOW?

The earliest fossils that scientists have found are single-celled organisms.

All fossils together are called the **fossil record**. The picture scientists have of evolution from fossil evidence is not entirely complete, but it shows that life on Earth has existed for billions of years. Fossils also show that life has changed during that time.

The fossil record tells scientists about evolution in several ways. It provides evidence of organisms that lived in the past but are now extinct. It also shows that not every organism alive today existed in the past. Fossils provide evidence that the physical complexity of organisms has changed gradually, becoming more complex.

How do paleontologists determine how old a fossil is? During the course of millions of years, Earth's rocks form layers called **strata**. The strata act as a timeline. Its top layers are the most recent, while the deeper layers were formed in older time periods. Often, fossils are buried in strata. Fossils found in the same location can be placed in age order based on the strata in which they are found.

(Margaret W. Carruthers)

Strata with unique features can be used to compare fossil ages in different locations. To approximately date fossils, scientists also use a process called **radiometric dating**, which measures the **radioactive decay** of certain **elements**.

TRANSITIONAL FORMS

Some fossils show evidence of intermediate states between an ancestor and its descendants. This type of fossil is called a **transitional form**. Transitional forms in the fossil record show how organisms have changed through time. They illustrate an intermediate evolution stage of change or adaptation.

How Fossils Form

Fossils form in several ways. Most form when a plant or animal dies and is buried in mud and silt. The organism's soft tissues decompose and the hard bones or shells are left behind. For millions of years, **sediment** builds up in layers that press down on the remains. Dissolved **minerals** are brought into the sediment by groundwater and fill in tiny spaces in the bones. Pressure and chemical reactions harden the sediment into rock and the bones into mineralized fossils. The fossils remain hidden in the rock until they are brought to the surface by **erosion** or are **excavated**.

Transitional fossils help to fill in gaps in the fossil record. As scientists find more and more transitional fossils, they can refine and confirm evolutionary theories.

In one example, scientists found transitional fossils that show part of the evolutionary history of the modern whale. Around 55 million years ago, a group of hoofed mammals spent more time in the water, eating the ocean's abundant food. Eventually, these animals left land entirely and evolved into whales.

Pakicetus attocki is the earliest known ancestor of the modern whale. It was typically a land animal that lived on the edges of a large, shallow ocean about 50 million years ago. The *Pakicetus* does not look like a whale at all. But its skull, especially the ear area, is very similar to that of living whales and is unlike that of any other mammal. This provides evidence to link *Pakicetus* to modern whales.

DID YOU KNOW?
Today, scientists know that life has existed on Earth for about the past 3.5 to 4 billion years.

WORDS TO KNOW

estuary: the tidal mouth of a large river, where the tide meets the stream.

isotope: a variant of a particular chemical element.

homology: a shared physical feature from a common ancestor.

tetrapod: a vertebrate with two pairs of limbs, such as an amphibian, bird, or mammal.

Several transitional fossils show the evolution from *Pakicetus* to modern whales. One of these transitional forms is *Ambulocetus*. Fossils of *Ambulocetus* provide evidence that it lived more in the water. Its legs are shorter, while its hands and feet are enlarged like paddles. *Ambulocetus's* tail is also longer and more muscular than *Pakicetus's* tail. The hypothesis that *Ambulocetus* lived more in water is also supported by where the fossils were found—sediment that was probably once an ancient **estuary**.

In addition, scientists have analyzed the **isotopes** of oxygen in *Ambulocetus's* bones. Saltwater and freshwater have different ratios of oxygen isotopes. By studying the oxygen isotopes in *Ambulocetus's* bones and teeth, scientists can learn about the type of water the animal drank. The isotopes showed that *Ambulocetus* most likely drank both saltwater and freshwater. This fits the hypothesis that it lived in estuaries or bays that linked freshwater and the ocean. By studying the whale's transitional fossils, scientists have learned much about the evolution of the modern whale.

Fishapod

Millions of years ago, animals that lived in the sea began to venture on land. *Tiktaalik roseae*, also known as fishapod, is a 375-million-year-old transitional fossil fish. Discovered in the Canadian Arctic in 2004, *Tiktaalik roseae* has both fish and amphibian features. It has fins, scales, and gills just like fish. But unlike fish, it has a functional neck with shoulders that are not connected to its skull. And it has ribs. Ribs help with breathing on land. Scientists believe *Tiktaalik* lived in shallow waters close to shore about 12 million years before the first tetrapods. Finding this transitional fossil, scientists are able to learn more about when the first fish moved onto land.

FINDING THE SIMILARITIES

Have you ever noticed that you and your cousin have the same ears? The two of you share a trait that you inherited from a common ancestor—perhaps your grandfather. If two or more species share a unique physical feature, they, too, might have inherited it from a common ancestor.

Physical features that are shared from a common ancestor are called **homologies**. The forelimb in vertebrates with legs is an example of a homology. Birds, rabbits, frogs, and lizards all have different forelimbs. Each animal's forelimb has adapted to its particular environment and lifestyle. At the same time, the different forelimbs are made from the same set of bones—the humerus, the radius, and the ulna. These same bones are found in fossils of *Eusthenopteron*, an extinct transitional animal. This homology provides evidence that these species share a common ancestor.

DID YOU KNOW?

To find physical homologies, scientists study an organism's anatomy and compare it to that of other organisms.

Organisms that are closely related usually have very similar anatomies. Sometimes, these similarities are easy to identify. Other times, they are difficult.

For example, did you know that whales and hummingbirds have a common ancestor? The proof is in their anatomy! Both animals have a **tetrapod** skeleton inherited from a common ancestor. During the course of millions of years, their bodies and lifestyles have adapted in different ways through natural selection. As a result, these animals look very different. Yet their skeletons have remained very similar. In fact, nearly every bone in one species matches an equivalent bone in the other.

WORDS TO KNOW

vestigial structure: a body structure that has no current function and is left over from a past ancestor.

embryo: an unborn or unhatched offspring in the process of development.

cellular: having to do with cells.

molecular: having to do with molecules, the groups of atoms bound together to form everything.

relative dating: estimating the age of something relative to another object.

Vestigial structures can also provide clues about evolution. A vestigial structure is one that has no apparent function and is left over from a past ancestor that did use it. For example, several animals, including pigs, cattle, deer, and dogs, have non-functional dewclaws. On your dog, the dewclaw is a like a thumb that grows higher on the dog's leg and has no role in walking. Dewclaws are vestigial features, leftovers from ancestors that had a greater number of functional fingers and toes.

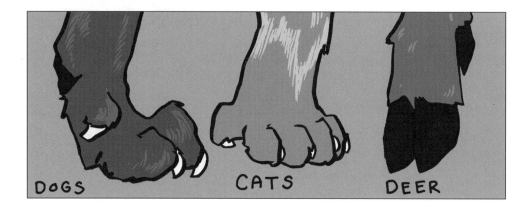

Sometimes, how an **embryo** develops can reveal clues about the evolution of an organism. An embryo is an unborn or unhatched offspring that is in the process of development. In some stages of development, embryos show evidence of ancestors' features.

For example, some whales have a full set of teeth. Other whales do not. Baleen whales have teeth in the early stages of fetal development. They lose their teeth before birth and are toothless for the rest of their lives. However, the development of teeth before birth provides evidence that baleen and toothed whales share a common ancestor.

Scientists also look for similarities at the **cellular** and **molecular** levels to find evidence of evolution. At the cellular and molecular levels, all living things are very similar. All organisms have the same genetic material, or DNA. They use the same or very similar genetic codes and processes for gene expression. Plus, all organisms are made of cells.

The function of all cells is also remarkably similar, with the cells of most living thing using sugars for fuel and producing proteins.

These similarities suggest that all organisms share a common ancestor. This ancestor had DNA as its genetic material, used the genetic code, had a similar method of gene expression, and was made of cells. Today's organisms inherited these characteristics from that common ancestor.

RELATIVE DATING

Evolution happens during millions of years. To determine the age of the earth and everything on it, scientists rely on **relative dating** and radiometric dating. Relative dating puts fossils in age order by noting their positions in rock layers, called strata. Remember, Earth's rocks build up layer by layer, with the oldest layers located at the bottom. Therefore, fossils found in these lower layers are generally formed first and are older than fossils found in higher strata.

DID YOU KNOW? If scientists can determine that strata A is older than strata B, they can reasonably conclude that a fossil found in strata A is probably older than a fossil found in strata B.

Scientists can determine the age of the fossils relative to each other—which one is older and which one is more recent—by noting their positions in the rock layers. Scientists study and compare strata from all over the world. This allows them to relatively date two fossils found in different locations.

Sometimes, certain fossils called **index fossils** help scientists determine the relative age of a rock layer. Some organisms lived for only a short period of time. While they were alive, they lived across a wide geographical area. Their fossils can provide a clue as to the age of the rock in which they are found. If you find a fossil near an index fossil, you can reasonably conclude that the two fossils are about the same age.

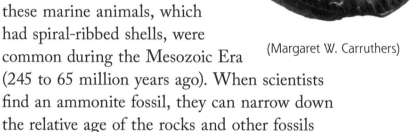

(Margaret W. Carruthers)

Ammonites are one type of index fossil. Now extinct, these marine animals, which had spiral-ribbed shells, were common during the Mesozoic Era (245 to 65 million years ago). When scientists find an ammonite fossil, they can narrow down the relative age of the rocks and other fossils found near it.

RADIOMETRIC DATING

Although relative dating can determine the age of fossils in relation to each other, it rarely pinpoints a specific age. For example, you might know that your grandfather is older than your dad, but how old exactly is your grandfather? That's where radiometric dating can be useful. Radiometric dating, also known as numerical dating, calculates age based on the decay of **radioactive elements**.

Nature is full of naturally occurring radioactive elements, such as uranium, potassium, rubidium, and carbon. Through time, unstable radioactive atoms decay and change into stable daughter atoms.

Hot, melted rock can come to Earth's surface through cracks in the surface and volcanoes. When this molten rock cools to form **igneous rock**, radioactive atoms are trapped inside. These decay at a predictable rate. Scientists measure the number of unstable atoms left in a rock and compare it to the number of stable daughter atoms in the rock. With these numbers, they can estimate when the rock was formed and how old it is. With this information, they can also estimate the ages of any fossils found in the rock.

However, most fossils are found in the layers of **sedimentary rock**, not igneous rock. Sedimentary rock is formed by deposits of sand, mud, and pebbles that eventually turn into rock. Sedimentary rock can be dated using radioactive carbon. Because carbon decays quickly, this process works only for rocks formed less than about 50,000 years ago.

To date older fossils found in sedimentary rock, scientists search above and below a fossil for layers of igneous rock or volcanic ash. They can date these layers using elements that decay more slowly, such as uranium and potassium. Once they date the layers above and below a fossil, they can estimate an age range for the fossil. This is known as **bracketing** the age of the rock layer where the fossil is found.

Molecular Clocks

Scientists are investigating the idea that some evolutionary changes happen in a clock-like manner. Under this theory, mutations build up in DNA at a predictable rate. If the mutation rate is reliable, scientists can use it to estimate the dates of evolutionary changes. The more mutations the DNA has accumulated, the longer it has been since it split from its ancestor's DNA.

BIOGEOGRAPHY

An organism's location on Earth can provide information about the history of life and Earth itself. Species that appear to be closely related usually live in places near each other. However, sometimes fossils of organisms are found far away from their places of origin. What can this tell us about the history of the organism and its migration patterns?

Today, **marsupial** mammals live in the Americas and also across the Pacific Ocean in Australia and New Guinea. Since these animals certainly did not swim the ocean to a new home, how did the two populations end up so far apart? To answer this question, scientists have turned to fossils for evidence.

Fossils of marsupials have been found in the Antarctic, South America, and Australia. Scientists believe that, millions of years ago, South America used to be part of a large landmass called Gondwana. Australia and Antarctica were also part of Gondwana. On this connected landmass, marsupials lived.

Then, about 160 to 90 million years ago, Gondwana split apart. The continents drifted until they reached their present locations, carrying the marsupials with them to their current homes.

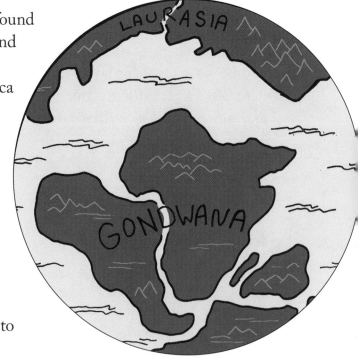

The Breakup of Pangaea

Millions of years ago, most of Earth's land was connected in a supercontinent called Pangaea. About 175 million years ago, Pangaea began to break up. Pieces of the supercontinent slowly spread across the globe, taking with them many different species. Organisms that had already evolved were spread worldwide. Other organisms evolved after Pangaea's breakup. They formed smaller, unique groups concentrated in smaller locations.

vimeo pangaea 🔍

DIRECT OBSERVATION

In some cases, scientists can actually see evolution taking place! Some microbes and insects evolve during relatively short periods of time. Scientists can view evolutionary changes directly. Drug-resistant bacteria and **pesticide**-resistant insects are two examples of modern-day evolution that scientists can directly observe.

In the 1950s, there was an attempt to **eradicate** malaria worldwide. Malaria is a serious and sometimes fatal disease that causes a flu-like illness, with high fevers and shaking chills. Malaria is caused by a parasite that infects certain mosquitos that transmit the disease when they feed on humans.

To eradicate malaria, officials sprayed a pesticide called DDT in areas where the carrier mosquitoes lived.

At first, DDT effectively killed the mosquitoes. With passing years, however, it became less and less effective. More mosquitoes survived.

In this case, the mosquitoes evolved through natural selection. A few mosquitoes in the population had genes that made them resistant to DDT. This gene arose because of a random mutation. When the DDT was applied, the mosquitoes with the DDT-resistant genes survived, while those that did not have the resistant genes died. The DDT-resistant mosquitoes could mate and produce offspring. For several generations, more DDT-resistant mosquitoes were in the population. Eventually, the population was mostly DDT-resistant mosquitoes.

Why was the mosquito population able to evolve so rapidly? First, a large population size made it more likely that some mosquitoes had random mutations that provided resistance to DDT. Secondly, mosquitoes have a short life cycle. This means many generations pass in a short period of time, allowing evolutionary change to occur. Bacteria and viruses have even larger population sizes and shorter life cycles. This allows them to develop **drug resistance**, such as antibiotic-resistant bacteria, at a very rapid rate.

There is one species that scientists are very interested in learning about—humans! In the next chapter, we'll explore the evolution of humans and learn how we came to be the way we are, and how we might evolve in the future.

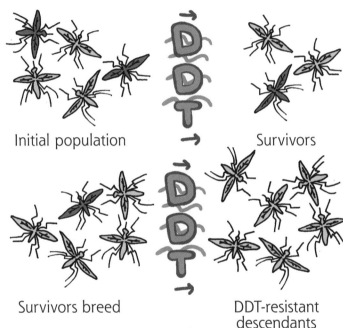

Initial population

Survivors

Survivors breed

DDT-resistant descendants

? ESSENTIAL QUESTION

Now it's time to consider and discuss the Essential Question: How do scientists learn about time periods that happened before written history?

Make Your Own Fossil

A fossil is the preserved remains or traces of animals or plants that lived in the past. There are two main types of fossils. Body fossils include the remains of organisms. Trace fossils are signs of organism's activities, such as footprints, tracks, trails, and burrows. In this activity, you will make your own fossils and examine them for clues about the organisms that made them.

❯ **To begin, gather a few items** that will make your fossils. You can pick leaves, flowers, your dog's paw print, shells, and other things.

❯ **Use clay to preserve your fossils.** You can either use clay that you already have or make your own using this recipe: mix together 1 cup coffee grounds, 1 cup flour, and ½ cup salt in a bowl. Stir in ½ cup of cold coffee until clay forms. Flatten the clay mixture on a piece of wax paper. Use a glass cup to cut out circles of clay.

❯ **Once your clay is ready,** press your item carefully into the clay circles. Gently pull the item away, leaving an impression in the clay surface. Allow the clay fossils to dry at least overnight.

❯ **Once dry, examine your fossils.** What can you learn about the organisms that made the fossils? Show your fossils to a classmate or friend. What can they learn about the organism from the fossil?

TRY THIS: Make trace fossils that show how an organism lives. What activities will you choose to show? How will you do it? What can you learn from these types of fossils?

Footprints of the Past

Scientists have found several examples of footprint trace fossils from early humans. One of the most famous sites where these footprint fossils were found is in Laetoli, Tanzania. There, scientists discovered footprint trace fossils of early humans from about 3.6 million years ago. The fossils were made when two early humans walked through wet volcanic ash. The footprint fossils show that the early hominins walked upright. The close spacing of the footprints also show that the early humans had a short stride and most likely had short legs.

Find Sidewalk Fossils

Sometimes, when builders pour concrete for sidewalks, streets, and driveways, people and animals step in the wet material and leave imprints. Leaves, branches, and other particles drop in and also leave markings in the wet material. These imprints are like fossils. In this activity, you will go on a hunt for concrete fossils and analyze them.

❯ **Take a walk through your neighborhood,** searching for impressions of leaves, branches, or other items left in wet concrete. Look for pavement where people or animals might have left footprints or where bicyclists have left tire tracks in the concrete.

❯ **Document your findings.** Make a map of your neighborhood and mark the location of each fossil you find. Take pictures or make drawings of each fossil find.

❯ **Study and analyze the fossil** to learn about the organism that made it. What type of organism made the imprint? How did you know? If you found tracks, what direction was the organism moving? How fast was it moving? How old do you think the fossil is? What do these fossils tell you about the organisms living in your neighborhood?

TRY THIS: Recreate footprint fossils in a sandbox. Dampen the sand until it is wet. Then walk across the sandbox at different speeds. Study and measure the imprints left at each speed. Have a second person walk through the sandbox. Create a chart for your data. How do the imprints change as your speed changes? What differences did you notice between the footprints made by the second person? How can this information help you when studying sidewalk fossils?

Exploring Half-Life

Radiometric dating is a way to date geologic materials. Different radioactive elements have different rates of decay. The element's half-life is the amount of time it takes for half of the radioactive element to change into another element. Depending on the isotope, the half-life of an element can be microseconds to hundreds of billions of years. In this activity, you will explore how half-life works and how it can be applied to radiometric dating.

❱ **Gather 100 pennies** to represent an atom of the radioactive element carbon-14. Carbon-14 decays into a stable daughter element called nitrogen. Its half-life is 5,730 years.

❱ **Dump the pennies on a table** and spread them out. The coins that show heads up represent atoms that have decayed and are no longer radioactive. Move them to one side of the table. Count and record the number of pennies left on the table with tails. These represent carbon-14 atoms that are still radioactive.

❱ **Gather the tail pennies,** mix, and dump again on the table. Identify the heads-up pennies and remove from the table. Count the remaining tail-side-up pennies and record. Repeat this process until all the pennies are no longer radioactive or you have completed 15 cycles.

❱ **Create a data table** from your records. Graph the information from the data chart.

✱ Based on your results, how many cycles did it take for half of your carbon-14 pennies to decay?

✱ If each flip represents 5,730 years, how many years would it have taken for all of the carbon-14 pennies to decay?

CONSIDER THIS: There are several types of radioactive elements that can be found in rocks on Earth. Why would scientists want to use more than one type of radioactive element to determine a rock's age? Why would they be interested in studying rocks from asteroids, the moon, and other planets?

Who Came First?

Relative dating gives an approximate age of an object compared to another object or event in history. Scientists use relative dating to determine the age of a rock or fossil compared to the age of another rock or fossil. For example, you can say that fossil A is older than fossil B but younger than fossil C. Using relative dating, scientists can tell if an object or fossil is older or younger than another event or object, but cannot tell the exact age of the object.

Relative dating is commonly used to compare layers of sedimentary rocks in different areas. Scientists also use relative dating to determine which fossil is older by comparing the rock layers the fossils are found in. When using relative dating in sedimentary rock, scientists follow several rules.

❯ Law of superposition: When layers of sedimentary rock form, older layers are on the bottom and younger layers are on top.

❯ Law of original horizontality: Sedimentary rock layers are deposited horizontally. Changes that tilt, fold, or break a layer happen later.

❯ Law of cross-cutting relationships: If an igneous rock or fault cuts through sedimentary rock layers, the **intruding** rock or **fault** is younger than the rock layers it cuts through.

Relative dating assumes that lower layers of rock are older than upper layers. Therefore, fossils found in older rock layers are expected to be older than fossils found in upper layers. The rock profile in one location can be compared to profiles from surrounding areas. If fossils are present in the layers, they can be used to **correlate** rock layers in other locations and determine the relative age of the rocks.

WORDS TO KNOW

intrude: to push in by force.

fault: a crack in the earth's surface that can cause earthquakes.

correlate: to relate rocks and fossils from one area with another area. Correlation is often used to determine the ages of rocks and fossils.

> **Using this information,** place the rock layers in the following diagrams in age order. Remember, always start by looking for the oldest rock. Then work your way through the rock layers from oldest to youngest. And don't forget what to do with the faults and intrusions!

TRY THIS: Using the information you have about the rock layers, write a paragraph about the geologic history in Diagram 3. What happened to create the cross-section you see in the diagram?

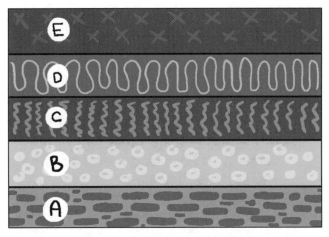

Diagram 1

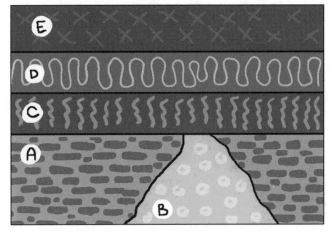

Diagram 2

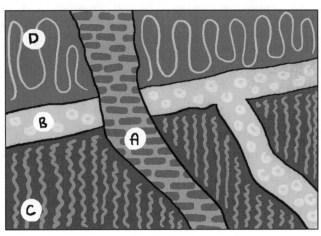

Diagram 3

Chapter 5

HUMAN
EVOLUTION

While many characteristics separate humans from other animals on Earth, we all have one thing in common—evolution! Evolution is not something that just happens to other animals, plants, and bacteria. It has happened and is happening to humans, too.

Human evolution is the process of change during a long period of time by which modern humans descended from our ancestors. Evolution does not change any one individual. Instead, it changes the inherited traits in a population.

? ESSENTIAL QUESTION

What can we learn about the present and future of the human race by studying ancient peoples?

Genetic traits that increase survival and the ability to reproduce are more likely to be passed to offspring. Parents pass genetic changes to their offspring and eventually these changes may become common in a population. Genetic change in a population can change what a species eats, how it grows, and where it lives.

Humans evolved as new genetic variations in early populations favored abilities to adapt to the changing environment.

Paleoanthropology is the study of human evolution. When paleoanthropologists search for the origins of human's physical traits and behaviors, they attempt to discover how evolution has shaped humans and our defining traits.

EVIDENCE OF HUMAN EVOLUTION

Scientists rely on several types of evidence to reconstruct the history of humans on Earth. Early human fossils and other **archaeological** remains are some of the most important clues about ancient humans. These fossils include bones, tools, footprints, and other evidence of activity left by early peoples. Most of the time, these human remains were buried and preserved. Later, they are found on the surface after being exposed by rain, rivers, and wind erosion. They can also be excavated by digging in the ground.

DID YOU KNOW?

Some people are uncomfortable with the idea of human evolution because it does not always easily fit with religious and other traditional beliefs about how humans and the world were created.

Scientists have found early human fossils of more than 6,000 individuals. Fossilized bones give scientists information about what early humans looked like and how their appearance changed with time. The size of the bones, their shapes, and markings on the bones from muscles tell scientists how early humans moved and how they held tools. Skulls shows scientists how the size of the human brain has changed. They can use the fossils to understand how well adapted an early human species was for walking upright or living in different climates. Fossils can tell scientists how quickly or slowly children of early human species grew up.

Scientists also study archaeological evidence, such as markings or objects that early people made, and the places where they are found. Stone tools are one type of **artifact** that provide evidence about how early humans lived, made things, and evolved.

Some of the earliest stone tools date back at least 2.6 million years.

Because stone is less likely to be destroyed than bone, many archeological sites have stone artifacts. These tools provide evidence about where and when early humans lived, how they migrated, and how they survived in different habitats. They also give clues about the **dexterity** and mental skills of the early humans.

Human Fossils

Many people think of dinosaurs when they think about fossils, but there are lots of human fossils to find! You can look at the collection of human fossils at the Smithsonian Museum of Natural History here. Can you find fossils that look similar to the bones found in our bodies today?

human origins fossils 🔍

Learn more about early human species here.

human origins species 🔍

Although fossils and other archaeological evidence are very important in learning the history of human evolution, scientists also use other types of evidence to recreate human history. **Phylogenetic reconstructions** help scientists understand how humans fit into the greater tree of life. Human DNA studies give information about how early humans migrated around the world and their connection to other species. For example, comparing human DNA with the DNA of Neanderthal, one of our closest relatives, gives scientists a better understanding of the relationship between the two species.

DID YOU KNOW?

The DNA of all modern humans is 99.9 percent identical, even as there is so much variation in how we look.

OUR PRIMATE COUSINS

Humans are **primates**. So are monkeys, apes, and lemurs. Even in the eighteenth century, Carolus Linnaeus classified humans with monkeys, apes, and other primates in his classification system. Although we have a lot of differences, there are several key physical and behavioral traits that link humans to these other primates.

Primates have well-developed hands and feet that have fingers and toes. They have opposable thumbs that allow them to grab objects. Their eyes face forward in the skull, giving them the ability to perceive depth and allowing them to judge distance. Their brains are large and highly advanced, which helps them control and manipulate their environments. Primates can also use complex language and communication skills. A highly developed visual center allows them to see different colors.

Primates can also run upright, using only their hind legs. They are born fully formed after a long **gestation period**. Mothers have a strong bond with their babies and care for their young for long periods of time. Primates are also very social and form strong bonds with family and friends.

COMPARING DNA

While scientists suspected that humans and other primates were closely related because of their physical and behavioral traits, DNA analysis adds further evidence. The number of differences and similarities in DNA between two species shows how closely they are related. DNA analysis has shown that the difference between human DNA and chimpanzee DNA is only about 1.2 percent. The DNA of the bonobo species, a close relative of the chimpanzee, also has only 1.2 percent difference with human DNA. This shows that humans, chimpanzees, and bonobos are closely related.

In fact, humans, chimps, and bonobos are more closely related to each other than any of them are to other apes. The difference in DNA between humans and gorillas is about 1.6 percent. Chimpanzees and bonobos show the same amount of difference from gorillas. Human DNA differs from the orangutan by about 3.1 percent and from rhesus monkeys by about 7 percent of their DNA.

All of this DNA analysis provides evidence for one fact—humans, chimpanzees, and bonobos are more closely related to each other than any of them are to gorillas or other primates. This DNA evidence supports the idea that the human evolutionary tree is part of the great apes' tree.

In 1871, Charles Darwin looked at the similarities between humans and African apes. He predicted that Africa was where the human lineage branched off from the apes' lineage. Africa, he believed, is where the common ancestor of chimpanzees, gorillas, and humans lived. Darwin concluded that human evolution began in Africa. More than a century later, DNA evidence supports Darwin's conclusion.

The Evolution of Bigger Brains

Millions of years ago, the brains of early humans were smaller and less complex. However, as early humans faced new environmental challenges, larger brains were an advantage. Larger, complex brains can process and store a lot of information. As early humans migrated around the world, they encountered new environments. Larger, more complex brains helped early humans interact with each other and their new environments. For example, during periods of dramatic climate change, a large brain able to process new information was a big survival advantage. This selective pressure led to an increase in brain size. Through evolution, today's human brain has tripled in size from that of early humans. Our brain is the largest and most complex brain of any living primate in the world.

bipedalism: the ability to walk on two legs.

DIVERGING FROM A COMMON ANCESTOR

DNA shows that our closest living biological relatives are chimpanzees and bonobos. But we did not directly evolve from chimpanzees or bonobos, or any other living ape for that matter. Instead, the human species and chimpanzees diverged from a common ancestor that lived about 6 to 8 million years ago.

DID YOU KNOW?

Every person living on Earth today is part of the same species: *Homo sapiens.*

We can trace our origins to Africa, where the earliest humans evolved. They lived in a variety of climates and environments. They evolved into new species or went extinct. About 2 million years ago, some populations began to spread beyond Africa into Asia. They faced new environments and climates. New species continued to evolve and eventually go extinct.

One of the earliest-known members of the human family were the australopithecines. One of the most famous *Australopithecus* fossils is called Lucy. In 1974, scientists discovered bone fossils that made up about 40 percent of the skeleton of a female in the species *Australopithecus afarensis.* They named the fossil Lucy. Scientists believe that Lucy lived approximately 3.2 million years ago. She was about 3½ feet tall and weighed about 60 pounds. She was also bipedal—she walked on two legs. Scientists believe that **bipedalism** evolved more than 4 million years ago.

The Missing Link

Finding the missing link between humans and apes is an impossible task—there isn't one! Chimpanzees or any other ape did not evolve into humans. Instead, both lineages have a common ancestor. The two lineages descended from this ancestor and then branched off, going their separate ways. So, instead of looking for the missing link, scientists are trying to answer the real question: Who was the most recent common ancestor? So far, the question remains unanswered.

About 200,000 years ago, a new species evolved in Africa called *Homo sapiens*. This species was the first modern humans, the ancestors of everyone alive today. We can all trace our DNA back to these early *Homo sapiens*. As time passed, populations of *Homo sapiens* spread beyond Africa. They moved into western Asia and Europe. There, they faced new climates and environments.

Homo sapiens are an adaptable species. As they moved around the world, they developed different skin and hair colors to adapt to different environments. Our ability to use our traits to meet new challenges enabled *Homo sapiens* to survive while other early human species became extinct. Modern humans spread around the world. About 17,000 years ago, *Homo sapiens* could be found worldwide. They were also the only surviving human species.

HI? HI!

Have you ever heard a gorilla roar or monkeys chatter? Many primates use a variety of sounds to communicate with each other. Gorillas and chimpanzees, some of human's closest relatives, can even learn sign language to communicate. What makes humans different is our use of rich and complex language.

Language allows us to record information, imagine different scenarios, and express complex ideas. This is a human trait that makes us different from other primates. Scientists are not sure when humans started talking, but they believe the use of language is a fairly recent event in the history of human evolution.

Spoken language does not create fossils, so there are very few clues about when early humans began to speak. However, some of the objects that humans made, as far back as 350,000 years ago, were complex enough that they probably required spoken language.

Sumerian writing from about 3100 and 2900 **BCE**

Different Skin Colors

Why do people from different parts of the world have differently colored skin? Different skin colors are an adaptation to different environments. Skin that was darker provided better protection against the sun's damaging rays. It also prevented the sunlight from stripping away folic acid, a nutrient that is needed for the healthy development of unborn babies. **Melanin**, the skin's brown pigment, is a natural sunscreen. People with more melanin in the skin who lived in tropical environments were better able to survive the harmful effects of the sun and preserve needed folic acid. But some sunlight is beneficial to humans. In colder environments with less sunlight, people with lighter skin had an advantage because they were better able to absorb what they needed. In these places, natural selection favored lighter skin.

As early humans evolved to speak, changes occurred in their anatomy. The voice box dropped lower in the throat. The area above the vocal cords grew longer, allowing them to make a wide variety of sounds.

There is a little more evidence for the development of writing and when it happened. Around 8,000 years ago, humans used symbols to represent words and ideas. Later, traditional forms of writing emerged.

DID YOU KNOW?

Scientists have found fossils in Africa that show the first 4 million years of human evolution took place in Africa.

OUR FAMILY TREE

For a long time, many people believed that there was a single line of human evolution. One species evolved into the next species, until reaching today's modern *Homo sapiens*. Today, we know this is not true. Like other mammals, humans are part of a large family tree. Fossils show that the human family tree has many branches and long roots. Most scientists recognize about 15 to 20 different species of early humans. More branches are being discovered all the time.

In fact, since the discovery of Lucy in 1974, the human evolutionary tree has nearly doubled its number of branches and its length of time. During some time periods, three or four early human species lived at the same time. Today, *Homo sapiens* are the only surviving human species.

While most scientists agree that there is a human evolutionary tree, they disagree on the tree's size and shape. How many branches are there? How are those branches connected?

Scientists also debate how to identify and classify different early human species and the factors that influenced the evolution and eventual extinction of each.

Most early human species, except *Homo sapiens*, have no living descendants. Instead, scientists must use fossils and other evidence to help them learn about these species and their evolutionary relationships. New fossil discoveries can help fill in the missing information.

DISCOVERY OF HOMO NALEDI

In 2013, two recreational cavers stumbled across some ancient bones in the Rising Star Cave, about 30 miles northwest of Johannesburg, South Africa. When scientists returned to the site to excavate the bones, they found nearly 1,500 fossils in total. These were bones from at least 15 distinct individuals.

In 2015, scientists announced that these bones were from a previously unknown species in the *Homo* genus called *Homo naledi*. *Homo naledi*'s fossils showed it had a mix of ancient and modern human features. It had traits similar to the genus *Australopithecus*, along with traits of the genus *Homo* and traits not shown in other **hominin** species.

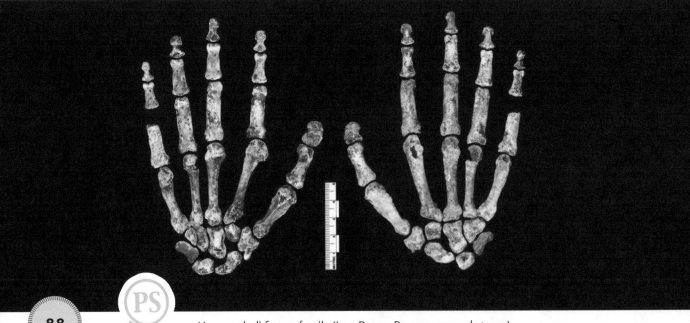

Homo naledi finger fossils (Lee Roger Berger research team)

Homo Naledi

Homo naledi was found in a cave that can be reached only through extremely narrow tunnels. If the explorers who discovered this cave had been just a little thicker around, they wouldn't have been able to squeak through the rocks to find what might be the most important archaeological discovery in a century! You can read more about the details of *Homo naledi's* discovery at this website.

new species of human ancestor 🔍

Its brain was small, about the size of an orange. Its hands were human-like, but the finger bones were locked into a curve, which suggests that the species climbed and used tools. *Homo naledi* stood about 5 feet tall, had long legs, and feet almost identical to our feet today. This suggests that they could walk long distances. Many scientists believe that *Homo naledi* could be one of the earliest members of the *Homo* genus.

DID YOU KNOW?

Many advanced traits in humans, including complex language, art, and **agriculture**, emerged mainly in the past 100,000 years.

There are many questions still surrounding *Homo naledi*. How old are the bones? How did they get into the cave? Scientists continue working to answer these questions and learn more about how *Homo naledi* fits into the history of human evolution.

The story of human evolution is not finished. Humans continue to evolve. Today, modern evolution is being driven by our culture, biology, and even the technology we have invented. Other animals are evolving, too, especially in response to changes in the environment made by humans. We'll learn more about these changes in the next chapter.

ESSENTIAL QUESTION

Now it's time to consider and discuss the Essential Question: What can we learn about the present and future of the human race by studying ancient peoples?

Mapping Early Human Migration

Scientists have found fossils of early humans around the world. These fossils have helped scientists study the history of human evolution and trace a migration path around the world. In this activity, you will follow fossil discoveries of several early human species and map their migration.

❱ **Explore the Smithsonian** National Museum of Natural History's online collection of early human fossils. You can find the collection online here.

human origins fossils 🔍

❱ **Select five species of early humans to follow.**
Use the website's sorting feature to find all of the fossils related to a species you have chosen. Study several fossils and create a chart to organize what you have learned about each fossil, including type of fossil, approximate age, and location found. Repeat for each species you have selected.

❱ **Plot the location of each fossil** on a small world map, using a separate color for each species. The colored points show the path of migration for that species.

✱ Looking at the map and your chart, which species overlap in time and location?

✱ What biological adaptations would you expect to find in each species based on their migration path? Explain.

CONSIDER THIS: Did the time period in which the species lived affect its migration path? Explain.

The Leakeys

While most scientists today believe that early humans originated in Africa, this was not always the case. In the 1930s, Louis Leakey began to search for human fossils in East Africa. Many of his colleagues doubted he would find anything. For several decades, Louis and his wife, Mary, explored sites in Tanzania and Kenya. In 1959, the paleoanthropologists uncovered the first of many early human fossils at Olduvai Gorge, located in Tanzania. This first fossil, classified as *Australopithecus boisei*, was called "Dear Boy" by the Leakeys.

Create a Timeline of Hominin Evolution

Different early hominin species have lived during the past 6 to 7 million years. Hominins include all humans and their extinct bipedal ancestors and cousins. Sometimes, two or more species overlapped and lived at the same time. In this activity, you will create a timeline of hominin evolution.

❯ **Using the Smithsonian National Museum of Natural History website,** create a chart that lists each known early human species and the date ranges the species lived on Earth.

human origins species 🔍

❯ **Using the information from your chart,** create a timeline of hominin evolution.

❯ **Using your timeline and the Internet,** investigate the following questions.

✱ When was the first hominin fossil found?

✱ When did bipedalism evolve? Which species was the first early bipedal hominin? When did the first evidence of tool use appear? In what species?

✱ Which was the first hominin to leave evidence of culture?

✱ What clues did hominins leave behind that reflect their **cognitive** abilities?

✱ What cultural adaptations allowed *Homo erectus* to migrate beyond tropical and **subtropical** environments into cooler climates?

✱ Which hominins lived at the same time? How do you think this was possible?

DID YOU KNOW?

In 1961, Mary and Louis Leakey's son, Jonathan, found a second type of hominin. The Leakeys named this individual *Homo habilis* or "man with skill." They believed this species had made the stone tools found at Olduvai Gorge.

CONSIDER THIS: What natural selection pressures do you think influenced the evolution of each hominin species? Did the different species experience the same pressures? If so, how did each respond?

WORDS TO KNOW

cognitive: activities related to thinking, understanding, learning, and remembering.

subtropical: an area close to the tropics where the weather is warm.

Comparing Skulls

In 2015, scientists discovered the fossils of a new species of early human, which they named *Homo naledi*. To learn more about *Homo naledi* and figure out where it fits into the human evolutionary history, scientists compare the bones and skull to those of other early human fossils. Scientists compare and analyze the similarities and differences between the species to understand their relationships. In this activity, you will study and compare the skulls of several hominin species.

❯ **There are several photos** of seven skulls available here.

❯ **There are four pictures** from different angles of each skull. The skulls are identified by their label "skull.xy" in which the "x" represent the species, while the "y" represents the picture view (f = front; r = right side; t = top; u = under). The skulls are in this order.

Indiana University skulls2 🔍

* b – female chimpanzee
* c – Cro-Magnon man
* d – modern human
* e – Neanderthal man
* f – *Homo erectus*, female
* g – *Australopithecus boisei*
* h – *Australopithecus africanus*

❯ **Compare each of the skulls.** Arrange them in order from oldest to youngest. What are the similarities and differences you notice in the size, shape, bone structure, nasal bones and openings, and jaw bones? What similarities and differences do you notice in the teeth—size, shape, number, and position?

* What features do the skulls have in common?
* What features are most useful for telling the difference between species?
* What changes have occurred through time? Explain why you think these changes occurred.

TRY THIS: How do you think human skulls will change in the future? Draw a picture of what you think a skull will look like in 5,000 years.

Bipedalism Advantage

You are bipedal, which means you walk using two legs. The earliest humans climbed trees and walked on the ground. This enabled them to move in diverse habitats and changing climates. Around 6 million years ago, one of the earliest humans, *Sahelanthropus*, left evidence that it walked on two legs. Did bipedalism help this species survive in the habitats near where it lived? In this activity, you will compare movements with two and four legs and analyze the evolutionary advantage it gave early humans.

❱ **How much faster can you run on two legs?** Time yourself running a short distance on two legs. Then repeat and time yourself using your arms and legs to simulate running on four legs. Repeat the experiment over different types of terrain, including pavement, grass, flat surfaces, and hills.

❱ **Chart your results and compare.**

✱ How much faster did you move on two legs?

✱ What evolutionary advantages did bipedalism give early humans? Write a paragraph to explain your answer.

	Two Legs	Four Legs
Pavement		
Grass		
Hills		
Climbing		

CONSIDER THIS: Why do you think other animals did not evolve to become bipedal? Explain your answer.

Chapter 6

WHY DOES
EVOLUTION
MATTER?

If evolution is the process of living things changing in the past, why does it matter for the future? Because evolution isn't just something that happened long ago. It is still happening, every day, all around. From the food we eat, the environment we live in, and our health, evolution continues to affect many areas of our lives.

Understanding how evolution works and how it has changed life in the past can be the key to predicting how life will change in the future. Around the world, human activities have changed and often harmed habitats, putting fragile **ecosystems** and wildlife in danger.

ESSENTIAL QUESTION

What do we hope to learn by studying evolution?

CONSERVATION BIOLOGY

Today, **conservation biologists** study how to maintain and restore habitats and protect wildlife. They provide scientific information for **sustainable** land use and water management. Conservation biologists are also using their knowledge of evolution and how it works to save species that are in danger of becoming extinct. Very small populations of **endangered** species face two dangers that may prevent them from recovering— **inbreeding depression** and low genetic variation.

> **ecosystem:** a community of living and nonliving things and their environments.
>
> **conservation biologist:** a scientist who studies how to maintain and restore habitats and protect wildlife.
>
> **sustainable:** living in a way that has minimal long-term impact on the environment.
>
> **endangered:** a plant or animal species with a dangerously low population.
>
> **inbreeding depression:** reduced biological fitness in a population as a result of the breeding of related individuals.
>
> **recessive gene:** a gene that is displayed with another recessive gene but is masked when paired with a dominant gene.
>
> **stillborn:** born dead.

WORDS TO KNOW

In small populations, two related individuals often mate. This practice of inbreeding might actually lower the population's ability to survive. Inbreeding depression occurs in small populations because two related individuals could each carry a copy of a **recessive gene** that causes a negative trait. When they mate, there is a greater chance the offspring will inherit both copies of the recessive gene and then display the negative trait.

For example, when a population of a type of snake called adders was isolated from other adder populations in Sweden, inbreeding resulted in higher proportions of **stillborn** and deformed offspring as compared to larger adder populations. This result is called inbreeding depression. When researchers introduced adders from another population into the small group, the small group recovered and produced more healthy offspring.

Low genetic variation is another threat to very small populations. Genetic variation in a population allows the population to adjust and adapt to changing environmental conditions. Without genetic variation, a population cannot evolve in response to changes in the environment. For example, a new disease can wipe out an entire population if no individuals have genes for resistance to the disease. This puts the population at greater risk of becoming extinct.

DID YOU KNOW?

Genetic variation can be restored only through the accumulation of many mutations across many generations.

As an endangered species' population gets smaller, it loses genetic variation. Therefore, conservation biologists need to figure out both how to save individual members of a species and to improve a species' ability to adapt and evolve to a changing environment, which starts with genetic variation.

Throughout the 1900s, people hunted the Florida panther in the southeastern United States. The few remaining animals clustered in the South Florida swamps. Because the remaining population of panthers was so small, the gene pool was limited. Genes that caused heart problems and reproductive defects were common. And because there was so little genetic diversity in the small group, these genes were passed to the group's few offspring. By the 1990s, there were fewer than 30 Florida panthers left.

Biologists predicted that the entire subspecies would be extinct by the early twenty-first century.

Extinction

Species go extinct for a variety of reasons. Sometimes, a random event such as a hurricane hurts a species so much that it cannot recover. Other times, another species wins the competition battle for resources. Even a new disease can wipe out an entire species. Extinction is an important part of evolution. Extinctions can provide more resources for another species or cause a surviving species to follow a new evolutionary path. During what's called a mass extinction, a large percentage of species alive at the time is killed off. With many species going extinct at the same time, mass extinctions can create opportunities for remaining species and change their paths of evolution.

In an attempt to save the panthers from extinction, conservation biologists released eight female cougars from a wild Texas population into Florida. Because the panthers are a subspecies of cougar, the two animals could mate and produce fertile offspring. The addition of the cougars tripled the number of Florida panthers. The offspring were stronger and lived longer. In addition, a 30-year-study showed that introducing the Texas cougars caused a significant increase in DNA diversity in the panther population.

Introducing the Texas cougars re-started the genetic flow between the two populations that had been cut off by human hunting.

Although the population is recovering, scientists say that the Florida panthers are not out of the woods yet. In order to continue the panthers' recovery, scientists are working to conserve the animal's existing habitat and allow it to expand its range, reducing more barriers to gene flow.

OUR CHANGING CLIMATE

Through Earth's history, our climate has changed naturally. Many of the past changes were caused by tiny variations in the earth's **orbit** that changed the amount of sunlight Earth received. Today, we are going through another period of **climate change** and **global warming**. This time, most scientists believe that climate change is caused by human activities. Global warming has been linked to rising sea levels and global temperatures, warming oceans, shrinking ice sheets and Arctic sea ice, melting glaciers, and more.

Scientists are studying how major climate change in the past affected evolution and life on Earth.

With this knowledge, they hope to better understand how today's climate change will affect evolution. How will it impact the diversity of life in the future?

Dr. Jennifer McElwain and her colleagues at the University College Dublin in Ireland have traveled to Greenland to collect more than 2½ tons of fossils. The fossils, such as 180-million-year-old conifer leaves, hold clues to Earth's past environments. McElwain studies the **stomata** preserved on the fossilized leaves. Stomata are openings in the leaf's surface through which a plant takes in carbon dioxide and releases water and oxygen.

LOTS OF CO_2 IN THE ATMOSPHERE...

...MEANS A LOW STOMATA DENSITY.

ONLY A LITTLE CO_2 IN THE ATMOSPHERE...

...MEANS A HIGH STOMATA DENSITY

McElwain discovered that the number of stomata per square inch on a leaf's surface can reveal clues about the atmosphere in which the plant lived. When carbon dioxide levels in Earth's atmosphere are high, plants need fewer stomata. Each stoma can bring in more carbon dioxide while releasing less water, giving the plant an advantage.

Therefore, during carbon dioxide-rich times, plants with fewer stomata will be more common. When carbon dioxide levels in the atmosphere are low, plants need more stomata to bring in enough carbon dioxide for survival. In these times, plants with more stomata will be more common.

Using this knowledge, McElwain studies the number of stomata on fossilized leaves to learn about carbon dioxide levels at different times in Earth's history. And because carbon dioxide levels affect global temperatures, her work is also providing evidence for how Earth's climate has changed over time.

McElwain is also using the knowledge gained from fossilized leaf stomata to investigate what caused different mass extinction events in the past. Her work is helping scientists discover how Earth's past climate changes have affected **biodiversity**. She hopes that better understanding this history will help scientists predict the future, including what species might be most **vulnerable** to global warming during the next 50 to 100 years.

EVOLUTION AND MEDICINE

Like all organisms, disease-causing bacteria and viruses evolve. Understanding how these organisms evolve and adapt to a changing environment can help medical scientists treat disease. Scientists study the evolution of drug resistance in disease-causing organisms in order to slow it. Learning about the evolutionary history of diseases may yield clues on how to treat them. And understanding basic evolutionary processes can help scientists better understand genetic disease.

Medical scientists are constantly waging war against disease-causing organisms in our bodies. When you get a flu shot, you receive a vaccine that builds up your body's immunity against the flu virus. But sometimes, you still get the flu. And next year, you'll need another flu shot. Why? Flu viruses travel the world, jumping from host to host. As they move through populations, the virus changes and evolves so much that the vaccine you received no longer works against it.

Bacteria and viruses such as the flu reproduce rapidly. As a result, they also evolve rapidly. Some bacteria can produce a new generation in only 15 minutes! With such short generation times, natural selection acts quickly on these organisms. In each new generation, the favored mutations and gene combinations are those that are advantageous against drugs.

During many generations, these disease-causing organisms adapt and develop drug resistance. By understanding how these organisms evolve, scientists are working to identify ways to slow their evolution and reduce drug resistance.

DID YOU KNOW? A vaccine is a tiny amount of a weakened virus that is put into the body. Just enough is given so that the immune system gets to work attacking the virus. The antibodies created protect you from getting the disease caused by the virus.

ANTIBIOTIC RESISTANCE

The introduction of antibiotics in the 1900s was revolutionary. Bacterial diseases such as tuberculosis and pneumonia that had previously killed many could now be cured with these wonder drugs. Antibiotics significantly reduced the number of people dying from many infectious diseases. However, because these drugs work so well, doctors have used them often to treat patients for a variety of illnesses.

This means many antibiotics have become less effective. During the past few decades, many strains of bacteria have emerged that are resistant to antibiotics. Bacteria that have genes or a mutation that makes them resistant to antibiotics have an advantage for survival. The antibiotic-resistant bacteria survive and pass on their genes, while bacteria without this advantage die off. After many generations, there are more and more of these antibiotic-resistant bacteria in the population. And because bacteria reproduce rapidly, this can happen very quickly.

As more bacteria become antibiotic resistant, they are much harder to treat and control than their ancestors were as little as 10 to 20 years ago. Antibiotics no longer work consistently to cure patients. For example, MRSA (methicillin-resistant *Staphylococcus aureus*) is a **staph infection** that can be resistant to a lot of antibiotics. As a result, not only can it be very difficult to treat, it is also becoming increasingly common.

In 1974, MRSA caused 2 percent of staph infections in the United States. In 2004, MRSA caused 63 percent of staph infections.

Today, doctors are treating MRSA infections with other drugs. However, these drugs are more expensive, work slowly, and have more side effects than antibiotics. By learning about how bacteria evolve, scientists hope to be able to control their evolution and use it to develop more effective medications and treatments.

Slowing Antibiotic Resistance

Evolutionary theory can provide strategies to slow down the spread of antibiotic resistance. These strategies include:

› Not using antibiotics to treat viral infections. Antibiotics work only on bacterial infections.

› Avoiding low-dose, long-term antibiotic treatment, which can leave bacteria survivors that have some resistant characteristics. Instead, short-term, high-dose treatment is more effective at killing all of the bacteria and leaving no survivors.

› Finishing an antibiotic prescription as scheduled to prevent any bacteria from surviving and adapting.

› Using a combination of drugs to treat a bacterial infection to more effectively wipe out the illness-causing bacteria, leaving no survivors.

› Reducing or eliminating preventive use of antibiotics on livestock and crops, which may lead to the evolution of antibiotic-resistant strains of bacteria.

THE EVOLVING HIV VIRUS

Scientists are also using evolutionary biology to discover new ways to treat or vaccinate against HIV (human immunodeficiency virus). HIV is a virus that can lead to the disease AIDS (acquired immunodeficiency syndrome) if left untreated. HIV attacks the body's immune system, the system that helps the body fight off infections. HIV can eventually destroy the immune system so much that the body cannot fight off infections and disease. There is no known cure or vaccine for HIV.

HIV is one of the fastest-evolving organisms known. A single virus can reproduce billions of times in a single day. To find a cure, scientists are studying how the virus evolves in the human body. They are also looking to learn why some people are resistant to HIV and how to control HIV's evolving resistance to drugs. They hope this knowledge will help them find effective treatments and vaccines for the deadly virus.

DID YOU KNOW? Although strains of HIV that are resistant to multiple drugs eventually emerge, the use of drug cocktails slows their evolution.

One way doctors are slowing the evolution of HIV is through the use of drug cocktails. When a patient begins taking an HIV drug, the medication stops some of the virus from reproducing, but some virus survives. These survivors have some resistance to the drug. Because HIV replicates and evolves so quickly, these surviving viruses are favored, and drug-resistant HIV strains emerge in the patient in as little as a few weeks.

By using drug cocktails, or a mix of several different HIV drugs taken together, doctors are slowing the evolution of HIV. With any single drug, it is likely that some of the virus will be resistant, survive, and reproduce. When the patient takes several drugs together, the likelihood of a virus being resistant to all of the different drugs at the same time is much lower.

AGRICULTURE

Understanding evolution can also help in agriculture. Using genetic variation and evolutionary relationships, farmers can improve the ability of their crops to resist disease. And understanding how insects and plant diseases develop resistance to pesticides can help farmers reduce crop damage. In these ways, understanding how evolution works can be an important part of securing the world's food supply.

Environmental conditions change all the time. When this happens, populations with large genetic variation will have some individuals that are able to survive. Through the process of natural selection, they will pass their advantageous traits to their offspring. The population will adapt and evolve to the new conditions.

However, when crops have low genetic variation, a change in conditions can lead to disaster.

In the 1800s, the Irish people planted potatoes that were genetically identical to each other. For some time, these potatoes fed the Irish people. However, when a potato disease swept through Ireland in the 1840s, the potato crops were destroyed. The ruined crops caused **famine** throughout the country. Biologists believe that the Irish potato famine would not have been as bad if the potatoes planted in Ireland had been more genetically diverse. Some potatoes would have survived and passed along their disease-resistant genes to later generations.

Developing Disease-Resistant Corn

Corn viruses cause damage to crops and hurt farmers' **profits**. Corn plants that are resistant to a variety of diseases can be very beneficial. Scientists are working to genetically engineer disease-resistant corn crops. Because the scientists cannot create new genes, they used disease-resistant genes that already exist. In the case of corn, scientists turned to the teosinte plant for genes. Teosinte is an evolutionary cousin of corn. As a result, teosinte genes could be used in corn. One species of teosinte, *Zea diploperennis*, from Mexico, carries genes for resistance to seven viruses that affect corn plants. Using these genes, genetic engineers have been able to develop virus-resistant corn plants.

Scientists are also using their understanding of evolution to slow the development of pest resistance to pesticides. One way to do this is by providing areas where non-resistant insects can thrive. Pest insects have short reproductive cycles and large population sizes. As a result, they evolve rapidly. If pesticides are widely spread, insects resistant to the pesticide will evolve.

Instead, farmers can provide **refugia**, which are fields without pesticides located near fields with pesticide-producing crops. Refugia provide havens for non-resistant insects. They can live there without significantly affecting the farmer's main crops. Because these insects survive and reproduce, the non-resistant genes remain in the population. Evolution of pesticide-resistant insects slows.

Through the study of evolution, we have been able to learn more about the story of life on Earth. And every single day, evolution continues. What will the future hold for humans and other species on Earth? Only time will tell!

ESSENTIAL QUESTION

Now it's time to consider and discuss the Essential Question: What do we hope to learn by studying evolution?

Antibiotic Resistance in Your Community

Many scientists are concerned about the decreasing effectiveness of life-saving antibiotics. In this activity, you will investigate antibiotic resistance in your community.

❯ **To begin, interview at least five people** in your community about their use of antibiotics. Some questions to ask include the following.

✱ Have you taken any antibiotics in the past year? Why were they prescribed for you? Did you have a confirmed bacterial infection?

✱ Did you take the antibiotic according to the instructions—in the proper dosage and intervals? Did you finish the entire course of antibiotics? If not, why not?

✱ Do you think it is important to finish a prescription even if your symptoms have disappeared? Why?

✱ Do you think doctors prescribe antibiotics too frequently? Why do you feel this way?

❯ **Next, interview local health professionals,** including doctors, nurses, and pharmacists. Some questions to ask include the following.

✱ Why is it important to finish all antibiotic prescriptions?

✱ How often does the doctor prescribe antibiotics? In what situations will they prescribe them?

✱ How frequently do you estimate the first prescription of antibiotics does not work and the patient needs a second prescription?

✱ How common is infectious disease in your community? Contact your local health department to get the latest statistics.

❯ **Using all of the information you have gathered,** prepare a presentation for your class. Do you think antibiotic resistance is a problem in your community? Explain your answer.

TRY THIS: Analyze the trend of infectious disease in your community. If possible, obtain records from 100 years ago, before widespread use of antibiotics. Then, compare these statistics to those from several points during the next century. What trends in infectious disease did you discover? How do you explain what you have found? Create a graph to illustrate your findings.

Create a Public Service Announcement

Antibiotic resistance is an issue that affects everyone worldwide. People can work together to slow antibiotic resistance by using antibiotics responsibly and as prescribed. To get the word out, you'll create a public service announcement (PSA) to help inform the general public about the threat of antibiotic resistance and what they can do to slow it down.

❯ **To start, gather information** about antibiotic resistance that is important for the public to know. You can find information at the following websites.

Centers for Disease Control 🔍

World Health Organization 🔍

U.S. Food & Drug Administration 🔍

* Centers for Disease Control

* World Health Organization

* U.S. Food & Drug Administration

❯ **With the information you have learned,** create a PSA. Your PSA can be a pamphlet, brochure, video, poster, or PowerPoint presentation. Make sure your PSA includes the following information.

* A description of antibiotic resistance

* The potential harm that can be caused by antibiotic resistance

* How natural selection impacts the effectiveness of antibiotic medications

* Recommendations on what people can do to fight antibiotic resistance

* What the government and other health agencies are doing to fight antibiotic resistance

❯ **Present your PSA to your class.**

TRY THIS: PSAs are just one way to reach the public. What other ways can you think of to educate people about antibiotic resistance? What type of message will be most effective?

The Importance of Genetic Variation

Genetic variation protects a population when something happens to change the environment or climate. Without genetic variation, a population is vulnerable to being wiped out by a new disease, change in conditions, or an environmental disaster. In this activity, you will demonstrate how genetic variation protects a population of toothpick fish.

❯ **To start, you'll need to gather several toothpicks** that are green (G), red (r), and yellow (y). Each toothpick represents three different forms of the gene for skin color in the fish. The green allele is **dominant** over all others, while the red and yellow genes are recessive to green and co-dominant with each other. The different gene combinations result in the following skin colors:

* GG: green
* Gy: green
* Gr: green

* yy: yellow
* rr: red
* ry: orange

❯ **Create two populations of fish.** One population has a variety of green, red, yellow, and orange fish. To make this population, take 8 of each color toothpick. Randomly match them up to create a gene pair for your fish. Count and record the types of genotypes and phenotypes of the fish in this population A.

DID YOU KNOW?

A population with genetic variation is more resistant to disease.

❯ **The other population has less genetic diversity.** It lives in a stream with lush green plants, which provide **camouflage** for the green-colored fish. Natural selection has favored these green fish, resulting in a population with fewer red and yellow genes. Create this population using 16 green toothpicks, 4 red, and 4 yellow. Match them into gene pairs and then count and record the genotypes and phenotypes in this population B.

WORDS TO KNOW

dominant: a genetic trait that hides the expression of a recessive trait.

camouflage: colors or patterns that allow a plant or animal to blend in with its environment.

❯ **Now, imagine an environmental disaster** has changed the ponds in which both populations live. Suddenly, the green fish no longer have an advantage in population B. In fact, the waste spill has killed most of the protective cover in both ponds, leaving sand and light-colored rocks, which provide camouflage for the red, yellow, and orange fish. Predators swoop in and devastate the green fish. They can no longer survive or reproduce.

❯ **Set aside all of the green fish from your ponds.** Record the genotypes and phenotypes of the survivors.

✱ How have the populations changed?

✱ Have any genes entirely disappeared?

✱ Which pond appears better able to recover from the environmental disaster? Explain why.

TRY THIS: Find and research a real-life example where reduced genetic variation is affecting a species' ability to survive.

Saving the Tigers

With fewer than 4,000 living in the wild, the tiger is a species that is vulnerable to extinction. During the past decades, tiger habitats have been destroyed and fragmented by human activities such as building roads and clearing forests. Fewer tigers can survive in these small, scattered habitats. And because tigers cannot spread as they once did, their gene pool is not mixing across the region. Genetic diversity has dropped significantly. The loss of genetic diversity puts tigers at risk of lower reproduction rates, faster spread of disease, and other problems. To save the tigers, scientists believe that increasing the tigers' genetic diversity is the key to its survival. They recommend conservation efforts that create ways for tigers to travel longer distances to breed with different tiger subspecies. By increasing the tigers' genetic diversity, scientists hope to keep tigers roaming for many years to come.

Saving a Species

Scientists are using their knowledge of evolution to help save species that are in danger of becoming extinct. Understanding how gene flow and genetic diversity affect populations can make a big difference in plans to save a species. In this activity, you will research an endangered species and come up with a plan to save it.

❯ **Use the Internet to research** a species that is vulnerable or endangered. Here are some helpful sites.

Amazing Amphibians 🔍

Animal Planet 🔍

U.S. Endangered Species 🔍

World Wildlife Federation 🔍

❯ **Choose a species to research.** Learn as much as you can about the species, including its habitat and behaviors.

* Why is this species threatened?

* What has caused the species to decline?

* How might this species become extinct?

* What would happen to the ecosystem where the animal lives if it becomes extinct?

* How would the loss of this species affect other organisms? How would it affect you?

❯ **Design a plan to save this species.** Consider the following.

* Is something in the environment or a change in the environment threatening the species?

* Would captive breeding help restore the population? Why or why not?

* Has gene flow been reduced? If so, how could you restore gene flow?

* Could you introduce a related animal to the population to restore genetic variation?

❯ **Present your plan** to save the species to your classmates.

TRY THIS: To explore more, consider that many endangered species, especially amphibians, live in your community. What endangered animals live in your state? Brainstorm ideas to help local endangered species.

A

adapt: to change in order to survive.

adaptation: a trait that has evolved through natural selection.

advantage: something helpful.

allele: a form of a gene.

allopatric speciation: the development of a new species due to a geographic barrier.

amphibian: an ectothermic animal with a backbone that lives on land and in water, such as a frog, toad, or salamander.

analogous: performing a similar function but having a different evolutionary origin.

anatomy: the structure of animals, plants, and other living organisms.

ancestor: someone from your family who lived before you.

antibiotic: a type of drug used in the treatment and prevention of bacterial infections.

archaeological: having to do with archaeology, the study of ancient people through the objects they left behind.

artifact: an object made by a human being.

artificial selection: the breeding of plants and animals to produce desired traits.

asexual reproduction: to reproduce without mating.

B

BCE: put after a date, BCE stands for Before Common Era and counts years down to zero. CE stands for Common Era and counts years up from zero. This book was published in 2017 CE.

behavioral isolation: different behaviors that separate two species.

biodiversity: the range of living things in an ecosystem.

biology: the study of life and living things.

bipedalism: the ability to walk on two legs.

bracketing: the process of dating the layers around a fossil to determine the oldest and youngest the fossil can be.

breeding: choosing plants and animals with improved characteristics to reproduce.

C

cell: the most basic part of a living thing. Billions of cells make up a plant or animal.

cellular: having to do with cells.

character: a group of heritable traits or characteristics that can be compared across organisms.

characteristic: a feature or trait.

chromosome: the part of a cell that contains genes.

clade: a group of organisms descended from a common ancestor.

cladogram: a type of evolutionary tree.

classify: to put things in groups based on what they have in common.

climate: the weather conditions in an area in general or during a long period of time.

climate change: changes in the earth's climate patterns, including rising temperatures, which is called global warming.

coevolution: when a change in one species causes a change in another species.

cognitive: activities related to thinking, understanding, learning, and remembering.

conservation biologist: a scientist who studies how to maintain and restore habitats and protect wildlife.

correlate: to relate rocks and fossils from one area with another area. Correlation is often used to determine the ages of rocks and fossils.

D

daughter atoms: atoms formed from radioactive decay.

derived character: heritable traits that evolved in a clade's ancestral history.

descendant: a person related to someone who lived in the past.

dexterity: skill in performing tasks, especially with the hands.

dichotomous key: a key to classification based on a choice between two alternative characters.

diverge: to separate from the main path and go in another direction.

diversity: a range of different things.

DNA: deoxyribonucleic nucleic acid. Genetic material that contains instructions that make us who we are.

DNA replication: the process of copying DNA.

drug resistance: the reduced effectiveness of a drug in curing or treating a disease or illness.

E

echolocation: the ability to find an object by sending out sound waves and listening for them to bounce back.

ecosystem: a community of living and nonliving things and their environments.

ectothermic: cold-blooded. Describes animals such as snakes that have a body temperature that varies with the surrounding temperature.

element: a substance whose atoms are all the same. Examples include gold, oxygen, nitrogen, and carbon.

embryo: an unborn or unhatched offspring in the process of development.

endangered: a plant or animal species with a dangerously low population.

environment: a natural area with animals, plants, rocks, soil, and water.

eradicate: to eliminate completely.

erosion: the process of wearing down Earth's surface, usually by water, wind, or ice.

estuary: the tidal mouth of a large river, where the tide meets the stream.

evolution: the process of living things gradually changing to adapt to the world around them.

evolutionary tree: a tree-like diagram that shows evolutionary relationships.

excavate: to carefully remove earth from a location to find buried remains.

extinction: the death of an entire species so that it no longer exists.

F

famine: a period of great hunger and lack of food for a large population.

fault: a crack in the earth's surface that can cause earthquakes.

fertile: able to produce or reproduce.

fitness: how successful an organism is at passing its genes to its offspring.

fossil: the preserved remains of a dead organism or the remains of an organism's actions.

fossil record: all fossils taken together.

G

gene: a section of DNA that codes for a particular trait.

gene flow: the transfer of genes from one population to another.

generation: a group born and living at about the same time.

genetic: traits that are passed from parent to child in the DNA.

genetic drift: a change in the gene frequency in a population due to random chance.

genotype: an organism's genes for a trait.

geographic isolation: when changing geography creates physical barriers between populations.

gestation period: the period of time an offspring is carried by its mother before birth.

global warming: a gradual increase in the average temperature of the earth's atmosphere and its oceans.

H

habitat: the natural home or environment surrounding an organism.

heritable: a gene or trait that can be passed from parent to offspring.

hominin: all humans, including all bipedal ancestors.

homology: a shared physical feature from a common ancestor.

homologous character: traits that are similar and were inherited from a common ancestor.

host: an animal or plant from which a parasite or other organism gets nutrition.

I

igneous rock: rock formed through the cooling and solidification of magma or lava.

immune system: the system of cells that protects your body against disease and infection. Includes white blood cells.

inbreeding depression: reduced biological fitness in a population as a result of the breeding of related individuals.

index fossil: the fossil of an organism that lived during only a short period of time. It can be used to date surrounding rock and fossils.

infertile: not able to produce or reproduce.

interbreed: to mate with each other.

intrude: to push in by force.

isotope: a variant of a particular chemical element.

L

lethal: capable of causing death.

lineage: a continuous line of descent connecting ancestors and descendants.

M

mammal: a type of animal, such as a human, dog, or cat. Mammals are born live, feed milk to their young, and usually have hair or fur covering most of their skin.

mammoth: a large extinct mammal that was hairy with a sloping back and long, curved tusks.

marsupial: a mammal, such as a kangaroo, that has a pouch where its young develop.

mating: reproducing to make something new, just like itself. To make babies.

melanin: a brown pigment in skin.

migrate: when an organism moves from one location to another.

mineral: a naturally occurring solid found in rocks and in the ground.

mnemonic: a tool, pattern, or association used to help remember something.

molecular: having to do with molecules, the groups of atoms bound together to form everything.

mutagen: an agent that causes change in the structure of a gene.

mutation: a permanent change in an organism's DNA.

mutualistic coevolution: when two species evolve together, with the changes benefitting both.

N

natural selection: the process that allows organisms best adapted for an environment to reproduce.

O

offspring: a plant's or animal's young.

orbit: the path the earth takes as it circles the sun.

organism: any living thing, such as a plant or animal.

outgroup: an organism outside the group being studied in an evolutionary tree.

P

paleoanthropology: the study of human evolution.

paleontologist: a scientist who studies fossils and the creatures that made them.

parapatric speciation: evolution of a new species because of an extreme change in habitat.

parasite: an animal or plant that lives on or in another plant or animal, feeding off of it, without any benefit to the host.

pathogen: a bacteria, virus, or other microorganism that can cause disease.

pesticide: a substance used for destroying insects or other organisms harmful to cultivated plants or to animals.

phenotype: the outward display of a trait. For example, curly hair and blue eyes are phenotypes.

phylogenetic: based on evolutionary relationships.

phylogenetic reconstruction: the process of comparing characteristics of modern humans with those of ancient humans.

polytomy: a node on an evolutionary tree that has more than two descendant lineages.

postzygotic barrier: a barrier that occurs after mating to prevent viable offspring.

predator: an animal that hunts another animal for food.

prey: an animal hunted by another animal.

prezygotic barrier: a barrier that prevent mating from happening.

primate: any member of the group of animals that includes human beings, apes, and monkeys.

profit: the money made by a business after paying all the costs of the business.

proportion: the balanced relationships between parts of a whole.

protein: a group of large molecules. Proteins are an essential part of all living things.

R

radioactive decay: the spontaneous breakdown of an atomic nucleus, which releases energy and matter from the nucleus.

radioactive element: an element that breaks down through time by releasing energy and turning into a different element.

radiometric dating: determining the age of rocks by measuring the radioactive decay of certain elements.

recessive gene: a gene that is displayed with another recessive gene but is masked when paired with a dominant gene.

refugia: an area without pesticide use that becomes a place where organisms can survive.

relative dating: estimating the age of something relative to another object.

reproduce: to make more of something.

reproductive isolation: when two populations lose their ability to produce live or fertile offspring.

reptile: a cold-blooded animal such as a snake, lizard, alligator, or turtle, that has a spine, lays eggs, has scales or horny places, and breathes air.

S

sedimentary rock: rock formed by deposits of sand, mud, pebbles, and other debris.

sediment: bits of rock.

sexual reproduction: to reproduce by mating.

similarities: things that are the same.

speciation: when a single species divides into two or more genetically distinct species.

species: a group of plants or animals that are closely related and produce offspring.

staph infection: an infection caused by staphylococcus bacteria, which is found on the skin or in the nose. Staph infections can be lethal if they affect major organs.

sterile: incapable of producing offspring.

stillborn: born dead.

stomata: openings on a leaf's surface through which a plant takes in carbon dioxide and releases oxygen.

strata: layers of Earth's rocks.

subtropical: an area close to the tropics where the weather is warm.

sustainable: living in a way that has minimal long-term impact on the environment.

sympatric speciation: the process through which new species evolve from a single species while living in the same geographic region.

T

tetrapod: a vertebrate with two pairs of limbs, such as an amphibian, bird, or mammal.

theory: an idea that tries to explain why something is the way it is.

trait: a specific characteristic of an organism determined by genes or the environment.

transitional form: a fossil that shows evidence of an intermediate state between an ancestor and its descendants.

tropical: the hot climate zone to the north and south of the equator.

V

variable: something that can vary or be different.

variation: a different or distinct form or version of something.

vertebrate: an organism with a backbone or spinal column. An organism without a backbone is called an invertebrate.

vestigial structure: a body structure that has no current function and is left over from a past ancestor.

viable: something that is capable of surviving and reproducing.

vulnerable: susceptible to emotional or physical harm.

RESOURCES

BOOKS

Ardia, Daniel, and Elizabeth Rice. *Evolution (Debating the Issues)*. Cavendish Square Publishing, 2014.

Currie, Stephen. *The Importance of Evolution Theory*. ReferencePoint Press, 2015.

Evolution: The Human Story. DK, 2011.

Huddle, Rusty. *Human Evolution*, Rosen, 2017.

Krukonis, Greg, and Tracy Barr. *Evolution for Dummies*. Wiley, 2008.

Johnson, Sylvia. *Shaking the Foundation: Charles Darwin and the Theory of Evolution*. Twenty-First Century Books, 2013.

Lew, Kristi. *Evolution: The Adaptation and Survival of Species*. Rosen Classroom, 2010.

Nye, Bill. *Undeniable: Evolution and the Science of Creation*. St. Martin's Griffin, 2015.

Wanjie, Anne. *The Basics of Evolution*. Rosen, 2013.

MUSEUMS

American Museum of Natural History
amnh.org

Carnegie Museum of Natural History
carnegiemnh.org

Harvard Museum of Natural History
hmnh.harvard.edu

University of California Museum of Paleontology
ucmp.berkeley.edu

RESOURCES

WEBSITES

Becoming Human
becominghuman.org

Evolution PBS
pbs.org/wgbh/evolution

Human Evolution 101
news.nationalgeographic.com/2015/09/human-evolution-101

Human Origins Project
nationalgeographic.com/explorers/projects/human-origins

Human Origins, Smithsonian Institution
humanorigins.si.edu

National Geographic Society
nationalgeographic.org/topics/evolution

Understanding Evolution
evolution.berkeley.edu/evolibrary/article/evo_02

ESSENTIAL QUESTIONS:

Introduction: What would the world be like if evolution never happened?

Chapter 1: Why is mutation important for evolution?

Chapter 2: Why are there different paths to speciation? Why is speciation important to continued life on Earth?

Chapter 3: Why is the structure of a tree useful for scientists who are classifying organisms according to common ancestors?

Chapter 4: How do scientists learn about time periods that happened before written history?

Chapter 5: What can we learn about the present and future of the human race by studying ancient peoples?

Chapter 6: What do we hope to learn by studying evolution?

QR CODE GLOSSARY:

Page 15: youtube.com/watch?v=0SCjhI86grU

Page 59: thinksciencemaurer.com/dichotomous-key-of-scientific-equipment

Page 59: gk12calbio.berkeley.edu/lessons/less_pinekey.pdf

Page 71: *vimeo.com/14258924*

Page 81: humanorigins.si.edu/evidence/human-fossils/fossils

Page 81: humanorigins.si.edu/evidence/human-fossils/species

Page 89: news.nationalgeographic.com/2015/09/ 150910-human-evolution-change

Page 90: humanorigins.si.edu/evidence/human-fossils/fossils

Page 91: humanorigins.si.edu/evidence/human-fossils/species

Page 92: indiana.edu/~ensiweb/lessons/skulls2.html

Page 107: cdc.gov/drugresistance

Page 107: who.int/mediacentre/factsheets/antibiotic-resistance/en

Page 107: fda.gov/ForConsumers/ConsumerUpdates/ucm092810.htm

Page 110: amphibians.org/amazing-amphibians

Page 110: animalplanet.com/wild-animals/endangered-species

Page 110: fws.gov/endangered

Page 110: worldwildlife.org/species/directory?directi on=desc&page=2&sort=extinction_status